Teaching and Assessing Phonics

WHY, WHAT, WHEN, HOW

A Guide for Teachers

Jeanne S. Chall
Professor Emeritus, Harvard University

Helen M. Popp
Former Associate Professor, Harvard University

Educators Publishing Service, Inc.
Cambridge and Toronto

The designs on the cover are representations of some of the letters of the Phonecian alphabet.

Cover and text design by Joyce C. Weston
Printed in U.S.A

Educators Publishing Service, Inc.
31 Smith Place
Cambridge, MA 02138
1-800-225-5750

ISBN 0-8388-2314-9

Contents

INTRODUCTION   v

1: *WHY* TEACH PHONICS?   1

Support from Research
Is Phonics Rote or Meaningful?
Students' Interest in Learning Phonics

2: THE *WHAT* OF PHONICS   6

What Kind of Phonics Should Be Taught?
What Teachers Need to Know About Phonics
What Students Need to Know About Phonics

3: *WHEN* TO TEACH *WHAT*?   16

A Sequence for Teaching
The *When* of Phonics

4: THE *HOW* OF PHONIC INSTRUCTION   21

Effective Phonic Instruction
How Much Time Should Be Spent on Phonics?
Textbooks, Workbooks, and Teacher-Made Material
Whole-Class, Group, and Individual Instruction
Objectives and Teaching Strategies
What is the Place of Sight Words?
Phonics and Other Word Identification Skills
What is an Effective Phonics Program?

5: WHAT ABOUT STUDENTS WHO HAVE DIFFICULTY?   29

Who Are the Children Having Problems?
What Should Be Done for Children Who Have Difficulty?
Students Who Overuse Phonics

6: THE PLACE OF PHONICS IN THE TOTAL READING PROGRAM — **34**

Language, Cognition, and Word Identification
Phonics and Whole Language Programs
The Relationship Between Writing/Spelling and Phonics
Why Do Some Phonics Programs Fail?

7: RESOURCES

Part 1. Phonic Elements and Generalizations — **40**
Part 2. Suggestions for Teaching Concepts About Print,
    Phonemic Awareness, and Phonic Elements and
    Generalizations — **66**
Part 3. Suggestions for Assessing Student Progress and
    Providing for Remedial Instruction — **89**

APPENDIX : WORD LISTS ILLUSTRATING DIFFERENT PHONIC ELEMENTS AND GENERALIZATIONS — **113**

Short Vowel Words
Alternate Consonant Sounds: Soft [c] and [g] Words
Long Vowel Words: With Final Silent [e]
Long Vowels at the End of Words
[y] as a Vowel: Long [i] and Long [e]
Vowels Followed by [r]
Silent Consonants
Words with Inflected Endings
Vowel Digraphs
Variant Vowel Digraphs and Diphthongs
Syllabication
Words with Prefixes
Words with Suffixes
Words with Multiple Affixes
Words Containing Vowel Patterns
Words Containing [a] Preceded by [w]

GLOSSARY — **149**

INDEX — **159**

Introduction

This book is for teachers, to help them gain a perspective on phonics. Research has shown that a teacher is critical to the success that students have in learning to read.[1] The teacher's knowledge of phonics is a key element of that success.[2] Teachers who understand the fundamentals of the relationship of print to speech will find themselves better equipped to help all their students—the ones who learn phonics almost by themselves, those who make normal progress, and those who, for one reason or another, have difficulty.

Teaching phonics seems to go in and out of favor in American schools. We have just gone through a period of about fifteen years when phonics was somewhat out of favor.[3] Consequently, phonics was not a part of the preparation of some teachers. Now these same teachers are being asked to teach phonics in their reading programs.[4]

This book is addressed mainly to those teachers, and to the countless others who seek a better understanding of phonics from its earliest levels—phonemic awareness—to more advanced levels—vowel combinations and syllabication. It presents research evidence on phonics and on phonic instruction. And it addresses the why, what, when, and how of phonics, giving the teacher the essential understanding needed to use phonics in a balanced reading program. Such knowledge is needed by teachers who follow more direct teaching procedures as well as by those who follow less structured reading programs, such as whole language. For teachers who follow less structured reading programs, it is even more important that they be able to take advantage of opportunities to teach phonics informally.

We have tried to keep the quantity of the phonics to be learned as limited, as simple, and as uncluttered as possible.

The book is divided into seven chapters. Chapter 1 discusses *why* phonics should be taught, with support from research, students' interest in the sounds of language, and an understanding of what reading is.

Chapter 2 concerns the *what* of phonics—the phonics that students and teachers need to know.

Chapter 3 answers questions about *when* phonics should be taught—when to teach the different phonic elements and generalizations and in what sequence.

Chapter 4 deals with effective phonic instruction, the amount of time to spend on phonics, and the materials of instruction.

Chapter 5 is concerned with phonic instruction for students who have difficulty learning to read, and what to do for students who overuse phonics.

Chapter 6 discusses the place of phonics in the total reading program.

Chapter 7 elaborates on the *how* of phonic instruction in specific ways. It contains a list of phonic elements and generalizations sequenced for student instruction and expands that list with additional information to serve as a handy reference for teachers. It also includes practical information such as sample lessons, suggestions for assessing student progress, and remedial instruction.

The book concludes with an appendix of word lists that illustrate various phonic elements and generalizations, and a glossary of terms widely used in discussions on phonics.

The need to improve students' reading is more urgent than ever, and there is sufficient evidence that this improvement can be achieved. With an increased understanding of phonics, teachers can foster a thoughtful and enjoyable approach to student learning, taking advantage of interesting and appropriate moments for teaching. Teachers can help students not only to learn the essential phonic elements and generalizations, but also to use them in their reading and writing. This will lead them to true independence in reading and open doors to the richness of children's literature. It is our hope that this book will support teachers' efforts through imparting the knowledge, confidence, and inspiration they need as they guide their students in learning to read.

Notes

1. Jeanne S. Chall and Shirley Feldman, "First Grade Reading: An Analysis of the Interactions of Professed Methods, Teacher Implementation and Child Background," *The Reading Teacher*, 19 (1966): 569–575.

2. John B. Carroll, "Thoughts on reading and phonics," (paper presented at the meeting of the National Conference on Research in English, Atlanta, GA, May 9, 1990).

3. Jeanne S. Chall, "Research Supports Direct Instruction Models," and Kenneth S. Goodman, "Gurus, Professors, and the Politics of Phonics," in "Point/Counterpoint" *Reading Today.* December/January 1992–1993: 8–10.

4. Bill Honig, *How Should We Teach Our Children to Read? The Role of Skills in a Comprehensive Reading Program—A Balanced Approach* (Thousand Oaks, CA: Corwin Press, 1996).

Why Teach Phonics?

Learning phonics means acquiring a body of knowledge about the relationship between written and spoken words, skill in its use, and a positive attitude toward its application in reading and writing. *Why* should students gain this knowledge? Support comes from research and long historical use.

Support from Research

Phonic knowledge has been taught to those learning to read from the time of the Greeks to the present. Just as the Greeks found it useful to teach it to beginning readers, the research conducted in the United States over the past seventy years or more has found the same. The research indicates that students who learn phonics do better in all aspects of reading—word identification, accuracy of oral reading, and silent reading comprehension and fluency—than those who do not learn it. This is also true in spelling.[1]

The correlation between phonic knowledge and word identification is very high, and skill in word identification is highly related to reading comprehension. In early reading, students who are better at word identification attain better comprehension because word identification and decoding are the major tasks they face. Their speaking and listening vocabularies are above their ability to recognize printed words. Hence, as they improve in word recognition and phonics, they improve in reading comprehension. Later, when students meet many new words that are beyond their speaking and listening vocabularies, it is necessary for them to be able to identify those words (and of course get their meaning) in order to comprehend what they read.

Weakness in phonics and in word recognition also tends to lead to dysfluent and slower reading because misreading words causes readers to backtrack. Fluency and automatic word identification are especially necessary as students enter the intermediate grades, when they read more difficult texts about times and places that are less familiar, more removed from their immediate experience. Their reading materials contain more difficult ideas and more abstract and longer words. Thus, even if students' word identification skills were good for the primary grades, they face new hurdles. These hurdles are especially prevalent in content area textbooks, encyclopedias, newspapers, etc. In the English language, less familiar, abstract, and technical words are generally polysyllabic; students in the intermediate grades and beyond need to be able to rapidly decode (sound out) these polysyllabic words.

If readers have difficulty identifying words, they will lose the concentration necessary to attend to the meaning of the reading and also be less likely to infer meanings for the unknown words. Facility and ease in identifying polysyllabic words, and in inferring their meanings from a knowledge of prefixes, suffixes, and roots, help students with comprehension.

Therefore, although word identification and phonic knowledge enhance reading comprehension somewhat differently in the intermediate as compared to the primary levels, they have a strong influence in the intermediate grades, and beyond as well.

Is Phonics Rote or Meaningful?

In the various debates on phonics, it has often been said that phonics is not meaningful—that it is a form of rote learning without thought or meaning. In truth, if taught well, phonics is a highly meaningful pursuit, but the meaning is of a different sort than that of sentences, stories, and other connected texts. What is meaningful about phonics is the meaning letters have in terms of sound—they carry the information about the sounds to be made. The correspondence between speech sounds and letters, and the rules that govern these, are meaningful. It is sometimes helpful to view reading as encompassing two kinds of meaning—the meaning of the medium (the print) and the meaning of the message (the ideas). Viewed this way, we can say that phonics gives meaning to the medium, the print, while the meanings of the words and the syntax give meaning to the message.

The two meanings—the medium and the message—are, of course, related. Phonics helps students pronounce words they do not recognize immediately. They can get close to the sound of a word and, through the sound, to the meaning. Phonics is a kind of code-breaking. As in any code-breaking, it helps if the word being decoded is in the student's oral vocabulary—that is, if its meaning is known. Yet, when decoding a word whose meaning may not be known, phonic skills are also critical. Indeed, only with a knowledge of letters and letter combinations and the sounds they represent can the reader make a reasonable try at pronouncing less common words, proper names, place names, trade and product names, and scientific and technical terms. An attempt at "sounding out" the unknown word may suggest the appropriate meaning. If the meaning of the decoded word is not known, the student learns to check its meaning through context, the dictionary, or by asking someone.

To make phonics more meaningful, several kinds of practice are important, such as reading unrecognized words in isolation, in sentences, and in connected text, as well as in signs and labels. Reading unfamiliar names and labels provides challenging and often humorous practice in acquiring phonic skills and generalizations.

It is quite embarrassing to misread names of persons and places and to be unable to make further attempts at the correct pronunciation. Many people also have difficulty using a telephone directory since they seem to be unaware that the same name can be spelled more than one way, e.g., *Schwartz* or *Shwartz, Beverage* or *Beveridge*, *McDonald* or *MacDonald*. Children and adults who have difficulty reading and spelling names will also tend to have difficulty locating words they hear in a dictionary. Here, too, they may have to look for the word under more than one spelling.

Meaningful reading implies more than the ability to get meaning from reading stories. It also means a growing facility in turning printed words into their spoken equivalents. Further, growth in using the medium—linking letters and sounds—enhances the acquisition of the other meaning—the meaning of the message. Similarly, the meaning of the message enhances the meaning of the medium.

Students' Interest in Learning Phonics

Children play with language when they learn to speak words for objects in their environment: *cat* for that furry creature, *bed* for that place where we sleep, *cup* for that which holds our milk, etc., and they learn how to string words together to communicate. In learning to read, they learn another symbol system that is imposed on the spoken words—on the sounds in those words.

Children are excited about learning this medium of literacy—the letters, the sounds represented by the letters, how words are spelled, and the reasons for these. Indeed, even children of three or four are keenly interested in learning the letters, writing their names, and reading signs.

Interest in and early facility with the sounds of language (now called phonemic awareness) are also highly predictive of early reading ability. On the whole, those children who show early interest in letters, printed words, and stories turn out to be better readers. This early interest in letters, writing, and rhyming predicts reading achievement even better than oral language ability and intelligence.[2]

When taught well, learning the letters and the sounds they stand for is intellectually stimulating and challenging. Such learning offers children and teachers opportunities for problem solving and for making exciting discoveries about the written and spoken language. It is exciting to share in predicting and making inferences about the relationship between writing and speech. It is intellectually stimulating to invent different ways of writing the same spoken words, and to generate feasible pronunciations for the same printed words.

Our writing is alphabetic and the alphabet is the way we represent sounds in English. The study of phonics can give teachers and students a sense of the great intellectual feat of the development of alphabetic writing. According to historians, the development of the alphabet is one of the great intellectual achievements of mankind. Over four thousand years ago, speech was represented by written symbols that stood for ideas. It was a long time before writing represented speech sounds with an alphabetic system of writing. It is believed by many historians that most of the alphabetic writing systems used today evolved from one of the early ones.[3]

In a real sense, children who learn phonics can gain insights into the language that are similar to those of linguists who study the relationships between word pronunciation and spelling in alphabetic languages.[4]

Phonics is a study unto itself, valued by linguists, philologists, dictionary writers, and cryptologists, as well as by reading teachers. When used by children, its main purpose is to gain knowledge and skill in identifying words not recognized immediately. Enhanced by knowledge and skill in phonics, reading becomes more accurate and fluent, and spelling improves. Both reading and spelling are done with greater confidence and accuracy. The ultimate goal is for children to apply with ease what they learn in the phonics program to their own reading and writing—that is *why* we teach phonics.

Notes

1. For this research evidence see the synthesis of the relevant research from 1910 to 1995 by Jeanne S. Chall in the three editions of *Learning to Read: The Great Debate* (New York: McGraw-Hill, 1967, 1983; Fort Worth, TX: Harcourt Brace, 1996). See also:

Marilyn J. Adams, *Beginning to Read: Thinking and Learning About Print* (Cambridge, MA: MIT Press, 1990); David L. Share and Keith E. Stanovich, "Cognitive Processes in Early Reading Development: Accomodating Individual Differences into a Model of Acquisition," *Issues in Education,* 1:1 (1995):1–57; I. Y. Liberman and A. M. Liberman, "Whole Language vs. Code Emphasis: Underlying Assumptions and Their Implications for Reading Instruction." *Annuals of Dyslexia* 40 (1990): 51–77; Miriam Balmuth, *The Roots of Phonics: An Historical Introduction* (Baltimore: York Press, 1992); M. Mathews, *Teaching to Read* (Chicago: The University of Chicago Press, 1966).

2. Millie C. Almy, *Children's Experiences Prior to First Grade and Success in Beginning Reading* (New York: Columbia University Teachers College, 1949); Dolores Durkin, "Early Readers—Reflections after Six Years of Research," *The Reading Teacher* 18 (1964): 3–7; Keith Stanovich, "Romance and Reason," *The Reading Teacher,* 47 (1994): 280–291; Jeanne S. Chall, Florence Roswell, and S. Blumenthal, "Auditory Blending Ability: A Factor in Success in Beginning Reading," *The Reading Teacher,* 17 (1963): 113–118.

3. Miriam Balmuth, *Roots of Phonics* (Baltimore: York Press, 1992).

4. N. Chomsky and M. Halle, *The Sound Pattern of English* (New York: Harper & Row, 1968).

2 The *What* of Phonics

In this chapter we consider *what* phonics is—what the teacher should know and what the students should learn. We present only an introduction to the relationship between speech and print in the English language, not all that is known. We limit ourselves to what we believe teachers need to guide students, and what students need in order to advance to ever more mature levels of reading.

What Kind of Phonics Should Be Taught?

Over the hundreds of years that phonics has been taught, different kinds of programs have been preferred and used. Programs have varied in whether they taught parts of words first, then whole words; or whether they taught whole words first, and then their parts. Programs also varied in whether they taught vowels first or consonants first. Other differences included the kinds of instructional materials used—textbooks, workbooks, or teacher-made activities. Classroom organization has also varied—from whole class to small group or individual instruction. (See Chapter 4.) But the variation that has received the most attention and has been researched most extensively through the years is whether phonic instruction should be systematic, explicit, and direct or whether it should be informal, incidental, and indirect. We discuss these differences below and include some of the research evidence for each.

Systematic, Explicit, Direct Phonic Instruction

All three terms have been used as labels for teaching phonics systematically. In this approach, the teacher presents the letter-sound correspondences. Individual letter-sound correspondences may be taught and then blended to form words (synthetic), or the correspondences may be taught by separating the sounds and letters in known words (analytic). In both cases, some instruction and practice is usually given in blending sounds to form words. Students learn to substitute consonant letters/sounds at the beginnings of words to form new words; for example, *cat* to *rat*, *can* to *man*. They also substitute final consonant letters/sounds, e.g., *cat* to *can*, *ran* to *rat*, and medial vowels, e.g., *tan* to *ten*, *tip* to *top*.

Most direct, systematic phonics programs are deliberate in style. They are explicit; they make clear to the students what is to be learned, how it is related to what was learned previously, and then they assist them in learning it.

Systematic phonics means that, on the whole, a "curriculum" is followed in teaching and learning phonics. The phonic elements and generalizations taught in the primary grades usually follow an order of utility and increasing difficulty. The more useful the phonic elements and generalizations are in identifying words, the earlier they are taught; the harder or less reliable they are, the later they are taught.

These phonics programs also give students practice in applying their knowledge of phonic elements and generalizations to reading new words and reading connected texts (stories, poems, and nonfiction).

Indirect, Incidental, Informal Phonic Instruction

Indirect phonics usually implies that students are expected to learn the letter-sound correspondences by inference from their reading of whole words and connected texts. Letter-sound correspondences tend not to be taught directly by the teacher, nor is there a phonics curriculum of increasingly more difficult phonic elements and generalizations to be learned. Usually, the teacher presents, incidentally, those phonic elements and generalizations that need special attention to the class, a group, or an individual, based on errors (miscues) made when reading stories or other texts.

What Is the Research Evidence?

Overall, the hundreds of studies (experiments in regular classrooms and in laboratories, and studies of students who experienced great difficulty learning to read) over more than seventy years, have found that students who learned phonics in the early grades—whether systematic/direct or incidental/indirect—did better in reading than those who received no phonic instruction; and that students who received systematic/direct phonic instruction did better than those who received incidental/indirect phonics.[1] The more recent research, in particular, gives strong evidence for a systematic/direct approach.

Further, the research evidence finds that the advantage of systematic/direct phonics is especially strong for students who are "at risk"—those who receive less literacy exposure and stimulation at home and those with reading/learning difficulties.

Why do systematic, explicit, direct phonics programs produce better results? Quite possibly because, being systematic, they can be monitored by the teacher. That is, the teacher knows what needs to be learned, when, and to what degree it has been learned.

Learning phonics through direct teaching requires less inference and discovery on the part of the students and is, therefore, within the grasp of more of them. When the teacher introduces the students to a phonics curriculum that is explicit and arranged in order of importance and difficulty, they practice major elements and generalizations, discovering and rediscovering the importance of what they have learned.

Although direct phonics is more effective than indirect phonics for most students, there are individual differences. Some children who have difficulty with what is now referred to as phonemic awareness (i.e., identifying rhymes and beginning sounds, segmenting words into sounds, and blending separate sounds to form words) may find it difficult to start with a systematic/direct phonics program. What they need is a more gradual approach to phonics using whole words first. They may thus be helped to see and hear differences in words, while working on phonemic tasks at the same time—identifying rhymes and beginning sounds. But even for these children, regular systematic phonic instruction is usually best after they develop some phonemic awareness. (See Chapter 7, pages 68–70, for specific suggestions for developing phonemic awareness and beginning phonic skills.)

What Does Experience Tell Us?

Our experience has been that beginning teachers, or those who do not feel secure about the phonics of English, do better when they use a systematic, direct, explicit approach with their students. As with all teaching, it is harder for students to acquire knowledge and skills from informal, unstructured procedures than from more formal ones. Also, it takes considerable knowledge and skill on the part of the teacher to ascertain the needs as well as the strengths and weaknesses of students. It is difficult to know if inferences about letter-sound relationships are made correctly when the student reads connected texts—especially when the reading is done silently. It is also difficult to know if a student is applying phonic knowledge and skills.

We have also found from classroom observations that a systematic, direct approach works better than an indirect approach in large classes. Similarly, we have observed that students at risk, who are either in clinical or classroom settings, do better with a systematic, direct approach. Traditional remedial reading programs as well as the newer programs, such as Reading Recovery, include teaching some form of phonics or word analysis. It is important to note that when more direct, systematic phonic instruction was substituted for the more informal, incidental teaching, it produced significantly better results, even for Reading Recovery.[2]

What Teachers Need to Know about Phonics

About the Spelling and Sounds of English

English orthography is alphabetic; letters are used to represent the sounds of words, not their meanings. Our alphabet has twenty-six letters which are used singly and in combination to represent about forty-four different sounds, or phonemes, in the language. Often the same letters represent different sounds (e.g., [ch] in *chip*, *choir*, and *machine*). And different letters may represent the same sound (e.g., [ai] in *maid*, [ay] in *may*, and [a] with a final [e] as a marker in *make*).* Spelling-to-sound correspondences in English are therefore more complex than in some other languages—Spanish, for instance, where one letter commonly represents only one sound.

In discussing the way writing and speech are related, linguists analyze the speech sounds first and then how they are represented in writing. This primacy of speech, the fact that letters represent sounds, is central to the reading and writing tasks. The reader translates the letters into sounds, either aloud or as "inner speech," and when a word is thus identified, the spoken equivalent to what is written can be given.

In studying a language, linguists determine which speech sounds are phonemes in that language. "Phonemes" are speech sounds that make a difference in meaning. For instance, /s/ and /t/ are significantly different; *sip* is a different word from *tip*. Thus the /s/ and /t/ are phonemes.**

---

*Throughout this book, we use the following symbols: [ ] refers to the letter or letter name, / / refers to the sound, and italics refer to the word.
**There are differences in speech sounds that do not make a difference in the meaning between words. For instance, the difference between /p/ in *pine* and /p/ in *tip* does not make a difference in meaning and is referred to as a phonetic difference of the single phoneme /p/. It is the phonemes that are of interest in the teaching of phonics.

In addition to phonemes, "morphemes" are important for the study of phonics. Simple words are morphemes, as are prefixes and suffixes, inflectional endings such as [s], [es], and [ing], and root words. A morpheme is the smallest meaningful unit of language. Thus, *cup* is a morpheme. Adding an [s] to *cup* changes it to a word with a different meaning. *Cups* has two morphemes: *cup* and the plural *s*. Adding [less] to *hope* produces the word *hopeless* which has two morphemes—*hope* and *less*, and it has a different meaning from *hope*. You will probably never use the term "morpheme" with your students, but knowing what morphemes are will help you to understand and explain changes in spelling, word meanings, and pronunciation. Morphemes are also significant in some syllabic generalizations, such as syllabicating compound words or root words and affixes.

Although English does not have a one-letter-to-one-sound correspondence, it is quite regular when we consider phonic generalizations and surrounding letter contexts. Your teaching will be more effective when you have knowledge of letter-sound relationships: which are consistent under what circumstances (generalizations), which are less frequent and less predictable but remain useful, and which are rare relationships. Such knowledge will help you call students' attention to a relationship they should know because it is frequent and consistent; you will know when to treat a relationship as fairly consistent but less common; and you will know when to encourage students simply to remember a given word because it contains a spelling-to-sound relationship that is very rarely seen. For instance, [ee] almost always represents /ē/ as in *feed*, and students should be encouraged to use that knowledge in decoding less familiar words such as *succeed*. In attempting words with the vowel digraph [ea], however, the situation is different. In this case, it is helpful to know that the most common correspondence is [ea] to /ē/ as in *meat*. If the long e does not yield a word (as in *spread*), the less frequent correspondence of [ea] to /ĕ/ should be tried. The [ew] to /ō/ in *sew*, or the [ai] to /ĕ/ in *said*, however, are very uncommon correspondences, and attention should not be called to them in these words.*

Part 1 of Chapter 7 presents the most essential letter-to-sound correspondences in the English language, those that are most useful to teach students in kindergarten through grades 3 or 4, and to those

---

*Exceptions to generalizations are not uncommon in high frequency words. Students will enjoy purposefully and playfully finding which words do not fit the phonics generalizations being learned.

in later grades who have not yet learned them. These letter-to-sound relations and phonic generalizations will also be useful to teachers who have had little preparation in phonics. Part 1 also incorporates a more extensive list of letter-to-sound correspondences to help teachers make better sense of some of the more unexpected spellings in English, which they can share with students as interesting insights, but not necessarily as generalizations they need to learn. It will also be of interest to teachers and students who make inquiries about the irregularities of the language.

What Students Need to Know about Phonics

Prerequisite Skills and Abilities

To learn phonics, one needs some facility with the spoken language and an ability to focus and concentrate.* Another prerequisite is the understanding that writing represents speech. Students who have been read to have usually acquired the understanding that the stream of speech can be divided into words and that these words correspond to printed words separated by spaces on the page. They will also know that printed words are read from left to right and top to bottom on the page. More difficult is the concept that the left to right sequence of letters within printed words represents the time sequence of sounds in spoken words. Finally, from these concepts stems the understanding that is basic to earliest phonic learning: the concept that spoken words have beginning sounds and that these correspond to the beginning letters in printed words.

The prerequisite visual abilities include an ability to visually discriminate among letters and printed words, remember the visual forms of letters and words, and track a sequence of words from left to right and top to bottom on a page. The auditory skills needed to learn phonics include the ability to detect rhymes and alliteration, hold spoken words and sounds in memory, and perceive minimal differences in spoken words (e.g., *pat* versus *cat*).

A more advanced prerequisite skill is the ability to blend separate sounds to form words and to separate sounds in spoken words. For example, when /k/ /a/ /t/ (sounded about a half-second apart) is heard, the student should be able to say the word is *cat*. Eventually, the student should be able to separate the word *cat* into the sounds /k/ /a/ /t/.

---

*It has also been observed that learning phonics helps most students improve their concentration.

Students for whom English is a second language may have some difficulty discriminating among sounds that are not found in their first language. Similarly, some dialects do not differentiate between certain phonemes; *pen* and *pin* may be said the same way, for instance. Confusion that may arise for students with dialect variations will be lessened considerably if the teacher is aware of such variations and gives additional help as needed.

These prerequisites, when they exist, make the task of learning phonics and reading easier. But they do not all need to be mastered before reading and phonic instruction begins. Some of these abilities develop as the student learns to read words and learns the correspondences between the letters and sounds. When a beginning reader is not progressing satisfactorily, however, it is suggested that these prerequisite skills be checked out. (See Chapter 7, Part 3, page 90–93 for suggested informal assessments of prerequisite skills.)

Phonic Concepts to Be Understood

The major purpose in learning phonics is to know how to translate a words' written form to its spoken form and vice versa, as an aid in reading and writing. To acquire enough of the skills and understanding needed to use phonics well, students need to learn which of the letters and letter combinations link to which sounds. They also need to gain an understanding of the following concepts:

- The same letters can represent different sounds.
- Different letters can represent the same sound.
- There are alternative ways to pronounce an unknown word.
- Rules (generalizations) may help determine the correct pronunciation, but they do not always predict the correct pronunciation for every word.

The Knowledge and Use of Letter-Sound Correspondences and Generalizations

The phonic elements and generalizations that need to be learned by students are presented in Chapter 7, Part 1. They are based on research by linguists concerning the nature of English phonology and orthography, the regularities and irregularities of spelling-to-sound correspondences, and research on the frequency of these correspondences in common and uncommon words.[3] In compiling Part 1 of Chapter 7, we also examined widely used reading textbooks and standardized reading and diagnostic tests. Overall, we have included phonic elements and generalizations that have the greatest utility for reading and writing. Essentially these can be summarized as follows:

single consonants

consonant combinations: digraphs (e.g., [sh], [th], [ch]), blends (e.g., [st], [pl], [br]), geminate (double) consonants (e.g., [tt] in *cattle*, [nn] in *manner)*

single vowels:

- short vowels in one syllable words: e.g., *cat, men,* etc.
- long vowels with silent [e]: e.g., *rate, kite,* etc. The final [e] signals that the preceding vowel is long.

vowels with [r]: [ar] as in *star,* [or] as in *for,* [ir], [ur], [er] as in *bird, fur, fern*

vowel digraphs (two vowels together):

- In many common vowel digraphs, the first vowel is long and the second is not pronounced: [ai] as in *paid,* [ea] as in *meal,* [ee] as in *feet,* [ie] as in *die,* [oa] as in *boat,* and [oe] as in *toe.*
- Other vowel combinations represent diphthongs that are "new sounds": [oi] as in *coin,* [oy] as in *toy,* [ow] as in *cow,* and [ou] as in *loud.*
- Some common vowel combinations may represent more than one sound, such as [ow] in *cow* or *crow,* [ou] in *loud* or *soup,* [oo] as in *boot* and *book.*

As students learn letter-sound relationships, they should also learn the generalizations relating to them. They should know the generalizations in Chapter 7, Part 1 so they can apply them correctly. That is, when students meet words that they do not immediately recognize, they will try "sounding out" the letters or word parts, according to the phonic generalizations they know, and then blend them together to form a word that makes sense. The value of phonics does not rest on learning all of the letter-sound associations, nor all the possible generalizations. That task would be overwhelming because there are so many exceptions. It is usually sufficient to learn a critical mass of letter-sound relationships and generalizations. These will usually lead to further learning on one's own. Often students who have grasped the concept that letters represent sounds and have learned some of the consonant correspondences begin very early to make inferences on their own as to which sounds are represented by which letters. The more they have learned about letters and sounds, the more they are able to infer on their own. This, in turn, leads to confidence in applying their phonic knowledge and to a freedom to try alternate pronunciations. If they are not right the first time, they are free to try again because they have the knowledge to do so.

Letter substitution strategies

Soon after some words are recognized at sight and the sounds of a few consonants are known, students can learn to read and write new words by substituting one consonant for another.

Suppose the student can read the words across the top row of Table 2.1. If he or she knows the sounds for the consonant letters in the left-hand column, he or she should then be able to read all the words in each column.

Table 2.1   Word Identification Using Consonant Substitutions

	cat	hall	night	gold	name
b	bat	ball		bold	
f	fat	fall	fight	fold	fame
m	mat	mall	might	mold	
r	rat		right		
s	sat		sight	sold	same
t	tat	tall	tight	told	tame

(See Chapter 7, Part 2 for additional suggested activities for learning the correspondences between letters and sounds, letter substitutions, phonic generalizations, etc.)

Skill and Efficiency in Using Phonic Knowledge

The Need for Practice

In order to use phonic knowledge and skills easily and confidently to identify new words, the student must gain experience with phonics in context. It is not sufficient merely to *know* the phonic elements and generalizations; students need to practice using them in con-nected text.

Skill also implies being flexible enough to try again when a spe-cific phonic generalization doesn't work. It involves applying phonic knowledge to reading and writing both individual words and words in context—in stories and other texts read orally and silently.

Attitudes

A positive attitude toward phonics helps students to learn and use it. In their early years, students "catch" a positive attitude from their teachers. They want to master phonics in order to give power to their reading. While it is true that phonic strategies are used less and less as the reader becomes more proficient, it is important to realize that they are needed even at the most advanced levels for reading scientific and technical terms, and the names of people and places. Phonic strategies are also important for new vocabulary in literature and other reading for pleasure.

Phonic instruction should help students have an open and playful attitude toward written and spoken words—breaking them apart and putting them together again, trying to sound out words this way and that, spelling unknown words and then checking in the dictionary for conventional spellings. This playfulness gives students the positive attitude and the confidence they need to use the knowledge and skills they are acquiring.

Essentially, the student needs to learn the letter-sound correspondences, the important generalizations relating to them, and skill and efficiency in using them. In addition, students should develop a positive and inquiring attitude toward written and spoken language.

Phonics, when taught as a body of knowledge, skills, and attitudes, is intellectually exciting and challenging. As students acquire phonic knowledge and gain facility with it, they can expand their vocabularies and read more advanced and interesting books. They can comprehend and enjoy what they read. And, as they gain confidence and grace in their reading, they gain confidence in themselves as well.

Notes

1. Jeanne S. Chall, *Learning to Read: The Great Debate* (New York: McGraw-Hill, 1967, 1983 [updated ed.]; Fort Worth, TX: Harcourt Brace, 1996 [third ed.]); C. A. Perfetti, "Language Comprehension and Fast Decoding: Some Prerequisites for Skilled Reading Comprehension." In J. T. Guthrie (ed.) *Cognition, Curriculum and Comprehension* (Newark, DE: International Reading Association, 1977); Marilyn Adams, *Beginning to Read: Thinking and Learning about Print* (Cambridge: MIT Press, 1990). See additional references on page 5, Chapter 1.

2. Sandra Iverson and William E. Tunmer, "Phonological Processing Skills and the Reading Recovery Program," *Journal of Educational Psychology,* 85 (1993): 112–126.

3. Richard L. Venezky, "English Orthography: Its Graphical Structure and Its Relation to Sound," *Reading Research Quarterly,* 2:(3), (1967): 75–105; Theodore Clymer, "The Utility of Phonic Generalizations in the Primary Grades," *The Reading Teacher,* 16 (1963): 252–258; Robert A. Hall, Jr., *Sound and Spelling in English* (Philadelphia: Chilton Books, 1961); Florence G. Roswell and Jeanne S. Chall, *Creating Successful Readers: A Practical Guide to Testing and Teaching at All Levels* (Chicago: Riverside, 1994).

3 *When* to Teach *What?*

A Sequence for Teaching

The sequence for teaching phonic elements to students that we suggest in Chapter 7, Part 1 is based on the combined research of almost fifty years—research on reading development, reading tests, and errors in oral reading.

Single consonant letter-sound correspondences are usually acquired before the consonant combinations, and consonant combinations are usually acquired at about the same time as single vowel correspondences, followed by vowel combinations. Skill in decoding polysyllabic words usually comes after the consonants and the vowels have been acquired.

Research on oral reading errors has found that fewer errors are made on the consonants, and more on the vowels. Also, beginning readers and older students with reading difficulty make more errors on the middle parts of words (where vowels are most frequent) than on word beginnings and endings (where consonants are commonly found).

Easier elements and generalizations are presented first, and the order we suggest is based on utility as well as ease of learning. The elements taught first are also the most consistent, and occur most frequently in the English language.

In English, as in other alphabetic languages, the consonant sounds are more prominent and distinctive than the vowel sounds and are therefore usually more useful in identifying written words. For example, it is possible to make a good guess in reading this sentence when only the consonants are used: L_ttl_ B_ P_ _p h_s l_st h_r sh_ _p (Little Bo Peep has lost her sheep). But it is almost impossible to make a good guess from the vowels alone: _i_ _e _o _ee_ _a_ _o_ _ _e_ _ _ee_. Consonant letter-to-sound correspondences are also more consistent. Twelve of our twenty-one consonant letters have a fairly common one-to-one correspondence, and some consonant combinations are also quite consistent (e.g., [ch] and [sh]).

Vowel letter-sound correspondences are more difficult to learn because most vowel letters represent more than one sound (e.g., [ea] in *beat, bread,* and *great*); and a given vowel sound may be represented by more than one vowel spelling (e.g., / ō / in b<u>o</u>ne, b<u>oa</u>t, and h<u>oe</u>), and each is often combined with other vowels to stand for other sounds. Although many of them become predictable when generalizations are applied, they are not completely reliable. They do, however, provide enough guidance to suggest a good approximation of the sound of the word. Therefore, consonants are taught first, followed by vowels. Often, several vowels will be introduced after a small set of consonants to permit students to read and write simple words.

It is also significant that most published phonics programs, and most basal reading series with a phonic strand, use a sequence similar to the one we suggest. A few programs start with vowels, but the most common progression is from consonants to consonant combinations; from single vowels (short, then long) to vowel combinations (digraphs and diphthongs); and from monosyllables to polysyllables. There are some differences within each of these categories since there is little empirical evidence to support a best order for teaching each of the elements and generalizations. Without such evidence, it is reasonable to teach first those single consonant letter correspondences that are discriminated more easily, both visually and orally, and whose sounds are most easily sounded in isolation (i.e., /f/, /l/, /m/, /n/, /r/, /s/, /v/, /z/). These are followed by the remaining single consonants. (The letter [c] representing /s/ and [g] representing /j/ are better taught later, after [c] to /k/ and [g] to /g/, because the former are less common in English words.) The sequence of consonants and vowels suggested in Chapter 7, Part 1 yields a large number of high frequency single-syllable words.

A few programs teach the long vowels before the short because the long sounds are the same as their letter names. But there is a drawback. Most long vowels occur in words ending in [e], and the rule of silent final [e] would therefore need to be introduced early. Also, a single vowel letter representing the long vowel sound is less frequent in English words. Therefore, most programs teach the short vowels before the long. As far as we know, there is no empirical evidence to support one or the other practice. The sequence we present has worked for us; other sequences have certainly been successful for other teachers. What is important is not so much whether the short or long vowel sounds are taught first, but how well they are taught and learned.

The *When* of Phonics

Phonic instruction should begin in kindergarten and continue, for most children, through the third grade. Some who have difficulty may need to continue through the fourth grade or higher. Some may need work in phonics only through the second grade.

A rich background for learning phonics is found among most kindergartners. Research on children's preparedness, or reading readiness, has been reported for over a century. Findings from the more recent research on early reading—emergent literacy and phonemic awareness—are quite similar to those of the early research. Very young children begin to develop a concept of reading. They know, for example, that print stands for speech, and they know the names of some letters. Many can detect and produce rhymes and alliteration. They are interested in reading signs, and in reading and writing alphabet letters, their names, and often other words that are meaningful to them.

A Phonics Program for Kindergarten Children

- The program will help students attain the concepts of "sentence," "word," and "letter."

- Most kindergarten programs also include letter naming and writing, rhyming, hearing initial sounds in words, and linking them with the initial letters in written words and with isolated letters.

- Writing one's name and learning to recognize the names of others are also useful and enjoyable activities. These give a sense of mastery and confidence to the students.

As these prerequisite skills are being acquired, specific phonic instruction can begin.

A Phonics Program for First Grade Children[1]

- Generally, most reading programs suggest that students know letter-sound correspondences for single consonants and consonant combinations (blends and digraphs) during the first grade.

- Often first graders are also taught the corresponding sounds for short and long vowels in the context of CVC (consonant-vowel-consonant) and CVCe (the rule of silent [e]) words and syllables.

- Plurals and verb endings—the beginning of structural analysis—are also usually taught in the first grade.

- Students come to understand how letter-sound knowledge can be used to "sound out" words they do not recognize. They practice using this knowledge in their reading and writing activities.

A Phonics Program for Second Grade

- During the second grade, practice is given in the different vowel digraphs and vowels followed by [r].
- Structural analysis skills are increased.
- Strategies to attack polysyllabic words are introduced— syllabication, recognizing prefixes, suffixes, and base words and how these are combined.

A Phonics Program for Third (and Fourth) Grades

- During the third and fourth grades children learn other strategies to attack unknown words; further work on longer polysyllabic words.
- Advanced work with root words, more difficult prefixes and suffixes, and more complex syllabication rules are introduced in the third and fourth grades and are continued in middle and secondary school.
- Students practice using their phonic knowledge and skill in reading and writing more challenging texts.

The order of learning need not follow exactly the order we have presented; it should be flexible to match students' needs and interests. The pacing will also vary. Some second graders, for instance, may be able to work with less common affixes and longer polysyllabic words usually taught to third and fourth graders. At the same time some third graders may need to review simpler vowel associations usually taught in the first or second grades. The important task of assessing student mastery of the elements and generalizations is left to the skill and knowledge of the teacher. (See Chapter 7, Part 3 for suggested assessment and review strategies.)

Adolescents and adults with limited reading ability (those who cannot easily read a daily newspaper) may still have difficulty with phonics, particularly with vowels and polysyllabic words. Some may lack the most fundamental phonic knowledge. It is, therefore, suggested that the teacher assess their needs and develop suitable remedial programs. (See Chapter 7, Part 3 for suggested assessments and remediation.)

Notes

1. Florence G. Roswell and Jeanne S. Chall, *Creating Successful Readers: A Practical Guide to Testing and Teaching at All Levels* (Chicago: Riverside, 1994); Jeanne S. Chall, "Patterns of Adult Reading," *Learning Disabilities: A*

Multidisciplinary Journal, 5(1), (1994): 29–33; Mary E. Curtis, "Development of Components of Reading Skill," *Journal of Educational Psychology,* 72 (1980): 656–669. Mary E. Curtis, "Intervention for Adolescents at Risk." In L. R. Putnam (ed.), *How to Become a Better Reading Teacher* (Englewood Cliffs, NJ: Merrill, 1996).

4 The *How* of Phonic Instruction

Effective Phonic Instruction

As noted earlier, phonics can be a part of many reading programs—whole language, literature-based, basal, or computer programs. Within each of these programs, certain principles are central to the teaching of phonics.

First, phonic knowledge is best achieved in a problem solving atmosphere. Phonic instruction should not be treated as a matter of rote learning and drill. Knowledge of letter-sound relations is best achieved in an open, questioning, thinking setting in which the teacher and the students question and ponder, are often surprised, and enjoy the task. When this atmosphere is encouraged, reading accuracy and fluency proceed at a faster pace, and the teacher and students are more satisfied.

Further, an effective phonics program should include specific instruction that encourages listening, writing, seeing, and saying. In general, instruction in new phonic elements and generalizations should be presented orally, with oral responses by students. The oral responses are sometimes given by the entire class, or a group, and sometimes by individuals. The teacher pronounces selected words to illustrate the letter-sound correspondences. Then students "sound out" and read the words orally to gain confidence and to let the teacher know that they have made the proper connections between letters and sounds. Independent activities including writing, reading, and activities such as those found in workbooks, or created by the teacher, are to be done only *after* the oral phonics work. (See Chapter 7, Part 2.)

Another principle is to provide opportunities for students to apply the phonic skills and knowledge they have acquired. When they fail to identify a word in connected text, it is often helpful to ask them to try again. At a convenient point, often at the end of the reading, it is helpful to show students how they might have corrected their errors by helping them recall the phonic elements and the generalizations involved. It is advisable to do this at a fairly rapid pace, in order to maintain interest in the story being read. Teachers should adapt their own procedures to the reading context, the age of the students, and their proficiency.

Oral reading activities, in which pairs of students, small groups, or even the whole class take turns reading a story, are excellent ways to apply the phonic skills and knowledge they have acquired. Students may also help each other. Rules to use when helping each other to correct mistakes (miscues) can be agreed upon by the students and the teacher. Be sure to clarify the rules that will be used to encourage trying, and learning from one's own and others' mistakes.

Finally, effective phonic instruction is enhanced by the teacher's manner in providing feedback, corrections, and encouragement. Progress, no matter how slight, should be recognized. To encourage students it is helpful to accept their success in recognizing parts of unknown words, even if they cannot identify the entire word. Applying phonics properly is not an all-or-nothing event. The classroom atmosphere should be one of freedom to try, and if incorrect, to try again.

How Much Time Should Be Spent on Phonics?

The actual time students spend with the teacher on learning phonic elements or generalizations, and in independent follow-up activities, will vary with the class or group. On the average, it should take no more than ten to fifteen minutes a day. On some days it may take only five to ten minutes. But since reading, writing, and spelling contribute to phonic skill, in reality, students practice phonics several hours each day.

The pace for phonic instruction should be brisk and energetic. The teacher should be a participant-observer, modeling student responses and taking turns with them to speed up the task.

During oral reading, the teacher should react to the students' successes and difficulties. If a student misses a word that contains a phonic element already taught, the teacher may help the student look at the word and quickly review with him or her the phonics that apply, providing this does not hold up interest in the story. Or the teacher may make a note of the word and help the student "sound it out" later.

After the oral work, the children may practice independently on a worksheet, or they may write words, sentences, or stories incorporating the new phonic elements or generalizations they have learned.

As students engage in the writing process, teachers may help during the editing phase by reminding them of phonic generalizations relevant to specific mispelled words. The richer a teacher's knowledge of the great variety of phonic generalizations and the alternate elements to represent a given sound, the more useful his or her suggestions will be.

Thus phonics is "taught" and "practiced" throughout the reading, writing, and spelling activities by encouraging and demonstrating its use.

Textbooks, Workbooks, and Teacher-Made Material

Most published phonics programs include textbooks or guidebooks for teachers and consumable workbooks for students. Some teachers have developed their own teaching program and pupil activities. Most teachers tend to use a combination of these materials.

Unfortunately, there is little research on which is the best practice. Our experience indicates that successful programs rely on all three—textbooks, workbooks, and teacher-made materials and activities. For beginning teachers, however, it seems that a teacher textbook, or guidebook, with workbooks for the children should prove most effective. With more experience, and for older students, teachers can rely more on materials and activities they develop themselves.

Whether the materials are formal (textbooks and workbooks) or informal (teacher-made activities), it is important that the teacher introduces the phonic work; that the elements to be learned are presented both orally and visually; and that students have an opportunity to practice orally under the teacher's guidance. Only after the oral instruction by the teacher and the oral practice and application by the students should individual, "silent" practice be given. When the individual practice is completed, it should be checked so that the teacher may identify those students who need additional explanation and practice.

Whole-Class, Group, and Individual Instruction

There is little research evidence on the most effective classroom organization for the teaching of phonics. Experience tells us that all have been and are presently used successfully for all kinds of programs—whether systematic or incidental.

Objectives and Teaching Strategies

Each time a teacher focuses on phonics—with one student or many, whether it is for two minutes or fifteen—the objective of the teaching should be clear. Is a generalization or a new letter-sound relationship being introduced? Is practice being provided to reinforce a relationship or generalizations previously taught? Is a new learning by analogy being encouraged? Knowing *what* is being taught will allow the teacher to evaluate whether it has been learned and will also allow students to gain a sense of accomplishment.

Various strategies (methods and materials) may be used in teaching and providing practice for phonic elements. Some of those given in Chapter 7, Part 2 are adapted from *Chall-Popp Phonics*.[1] They are presented as examples only, and we hope they will encourage teacher creativity. If teachers know *what* they want to teach and have words readily available that illustrate the element or concept, the possibilities for instruction are limitless. See the Appendix for word lists arranged to correspond with the phonic elements and generalizations to be taught.

What Is the Place of Sight Words?

The term *sight words* is commonly used to convey several different meanings. The first meaning is in reference to words recognized as wholes, by sight, without reliance on phonics, or decoding. These words may have been acquired through phonics or they may have been learned as wholes, and/or through reading them in context. But after repeated readings, they are all recognized at *sight* and are thus considered sight words.

Recognizing words at sight is really the ultimate goal of phonic instruction. Word recognition by "sounding out" is used only for words that are not recognized immediately at sight. And once they are read by sounding out, they can then become sight words as they are met again and again in connected text.

As one becomes a reader of greater maturity and efficiency, the number of sight words increases until the most advanced and skillful readers identify almost all words at sight, automatically. New low frequency words, technical words, proper nouns, trade names, and foreign names or words may need to be sounded out. But most words that are frequently seen in print become sight words since they are read over and over again in connected texts and are used in writing. The more often the words are read and written, the more automatic the recognition.

The term *sight words* also refers to words found in beginning reading materials that do not follow in all respects the expected letter-sound correspondences, e.g., *come* and *gone*. If phonic rules applied, these words would rhyme with *dome* and *bone* (long vowel preceding a final [e]). Many such words are among the most frequent in the English language, such as *the, was,* and *to*. And yet, although they are not spelled entirely as expected, there is some regularity in their spelling. If not recognized at sight, they are easily recognized from the consonant cues and the surrounding context.

A third use of the term *sight words* is for the 220 words on the Dolch List—words that make up about 75 percent of the words in primary reading materials and about 50 percent of the words in adult newspapers and magazines, e.g., *the, is, was, said, girl, boy, me, you,* etc.

There is considerable overlap in the second and third meanings of sight words. They both include highly frequent words that tend to have less regular letter-sound correspondences. Repeated exposure to these words in stories and books gives practice in identifying them as whole words, in context and in isolation, which increases the probability of their being identified easily. And thence they also become sight words in the sense of the first meaning above.

It should be clear that a good phonics program also needs to pay attention to sight recognition. In a real sense, fluent connected reading depends on fluent and automatic sight recognition and on the application of phonic knowledge. Wide reading provides the practice needed for both.

Phonics and Other Word Identification Skills
Prereading and Early Reading Strategies

The earliest attempts to read, it would seem, are global. Children use pictures, distinctive features of words, color, print size, memory—whatever cues are available. When the preschool child says "McDonald's" as he or she looks at the sign, or "Stop" at the red and white sign with its distinctive shape, it probably is not because of any awareness of letters or the printed words. This global approach to reading is typically concerned with the meaning of the word/sign or its context.

It follows quite naturally, then, that when children begin to attend to the written word, oral reading errors are characterized by word substitutions which tend to fit the general appearance of the word, its meaning, and the grammar of the sentence. Picture cues, semantic cues, and syntactic cues are most salient.

As readers advance, they learn that the sound of a word is based on its letters, and that the letters "stand for" sounds in the words they speak. In this second phase, readers learn the letters and the sounds they represent, and they use this knowledge to help them identify words and to write them. Word identification in reading text is characterized by an increase in attention to the phonic elements of the words. But as with all learning, this is not done perfectly at the start. The readers at this stage hesitate more as they try to use their newly acquired phonic knowledge to recognize the words. As they do this, they focus less attention on meaning, and make mistakes. These mistakes often reveal that the students are giving more attention to the letter-sound correspondences and less to the semantic and syntactic cues.

Finally, with greater phonic knowledge and practice, new words are identified by a combination of phonic and context cues—semantic and syntactic. Oral reading errors reflect the influence of both in this third phase of learning to recognize words.[2]

The qualitative changes described above tend to differ somewhat according to whether beginning reading instruction emphasizes the learning of whole words or phonics. Children whose beginning reading instruction emphasizes whole word learning tend to progress more slowly through these qualitative changes than children who learn phonics early.[3] However, all children seem to move through these phases in the same sequence regardless of the focus of their beginning reading instruction. Better readers progress through them faster. Less proficient readers progress at a slower rate and seem to persist for a longer period of time in substituting contextually appropriate rather than phonically appropriate words. Yet for most readers, the general progression seems to be from sole emphasis on meaning, to a greater concentration on phonics, to using a combination of phonics and meaning.

As readers become even more advanced, phonic strategies give way to quick sight recognition of most words. They use phonic knowledge only to identify words they do not immediately recognize. But when students read more difficult texts that contain a larger percentage of unfamiliar, long words, they will need to be proficient in advanced phonics, e.g., identifying syllables and combining them in polysyllabic words.

Syllabication

Syllabication refers to the separation of multisyllabic words into smaller units that can be decoded. These units can then be synthesized to form the spoken words. For this task polysyllabic words should be divided into separate syllables, with each syllable containing one vowel sound. Each syllable may contain more than one vowel letter, but the letters will represent only one vowel sound.

Many phonics programs do not include work on syllabication, teaching only the elements and generalizations needed to decode one-syllable words. One can argue that the rules for syllabication as an aid to pronouncing polysyllabic words are not very reliable. This is probably true. But certain rules, nevertheless, do provide a way to approximate pronunciations; and once approximated, the student is closer to identifying the polysyllabic words. (See Chapter 7, Part 1, page 58.) Knowing how to decode polysyllabic words is essential because reading materials in the third grade, and surely by the fourth grade and beyond, contain an ever increasing number of unfamiliar polysyllabic words.

Instruction in syllabication can start early, as early as grade 1, by calling attention to common compound words that are easily divided into separate words: *base/ball, in/side, some/thing,* etc. Other common two-syllable words can also be learned in the first and second grades: *chick/en, pup/py, kit/ten, win/dow,* etc.

The next syllabication tasks involve practice in recognizing and writing words of more than one syllable that have inflectional endings—prefixes and/or suffixes. Inflectional endings often make up a syllable: *tight/er, tight/est, skat/ing,* and sometimes even _ed_ as in *skat/ed.* Prefixes and suffixes help in word recognition and also in determining word meaning: _un_/tied, _re_/place, _dis_/please, hope/_ful_, large/_ly_, sleeve/_less_, _re_/pay/_able_, etc. At higher levels, less common prefixes and suffixes (some containing two syllables) signal both meaning and recognition: _semi_/rigid, _trans_/port, _hyper_/active, prefer/_ence_, deposit/_ory_, novel/_ette_, etc.

Most difficult to syllabicate are the less frequent polysyllabic words that are found in more advanced literature and popular fiction; in content area textbooks, encyclopedias, and other reference works; and in newspapers and magazines—words such as *international* and *governmental* (in social studies) and *hydrogen* and *organically* (in science). They are difficult because rules often suggest several alternative pronunciations and thus may confuse some students. Since the rules of syllabication do not always lead to accurate pronunciation, it is better not to spend too much time on learning rules and generalizations. Instead, it is best to have students gain insight and confidence by practicing how it is done. (See Chapter 7, Part 2 for suggestions.)

The best way we have found to teach and learn syllabication of long words is to be playful, correcting errors with cheer and laughing easily at humorous misreadings.

What is an Effective Phonics Program?

An effective phonics program helps students grasp the essential nature of phonics and provides practice in using phonic knowledge and skills. The phonic lessons should be designed to give students insight into the relationships between the letters and sounds, and how these relate to the way the words are pronounced and written. Thus it would teach the basic phonic elements and generalizations from kindergarten through about the third grade. It would help students develop skill in analyzing and building words based on that knowledge. Ideally, it would give the teacher information about each student's progress in developing those skills.

Programs are more apt to succeed if they do not try to teach every correspondence and every rule, if they provide plenty of practice in decoding single words and words in connected text, if they are flexible, if they give attention to whole word recognition as well as to phonics, and if students are encouraged to apply phonics when reading connected text.

An effective phonics program should complement a variety of other reading and language activities to give students practice in using the phonics they are learning. It should also provide activities for students to apply phonic knowledge and generalizations in their writing. Finally, teachers should also impart a sense of joy and power in the growth of each student's ability to identify and write unfamiliar words.

When less structured reading programs, such as whole language, are used, it is increasingly important that the teacher knows and understands phonics very well and takes advantage of interesting and appropriate moments for teaching it. This is also true for literature-based, language experience, and individualized reading programs. For those programs, phonics should be considered a significant factor in successful reading development. How well phonics is taught and how well it is integrated into the total language arts program is largely dependent on the knowledge and skill of the teacher—a strong challenge indeed!

Notes

1. Jeanne S. Chall and Helen Popp, *Chall-Popp Phonics* (Elizabethtown, PA: Continental Press, 1996).

2. Andrew Biemiller, "The Development of the Use of Graphic and Contextual Information as Children Learn to Read," *Reading Research Quarterly,* 6 (1970): 75–96.

3. Andrew Biemiller, "Relationships Between Oral Reading Rates for Letters, Words, and Simple Text in the Development of Reading Achievement," *Reading Research Quarterly,* 13 (1977–8): 223–253.

5 What About Students Who Have Difficulty?

Who Are the Children Having Difficulty?

Some children seem to learn phonics almost by themselves, with little instruction. Others find it difficult to learn, even when they receive good instruction; they learn slowly and with difficulty. Still others—in fact, most children—fall in the middle; they do well when given good instruction and ample opportunity for practice. Generally, this last group (and the first) can apply what they learn about phonics to their reading with little difficulty.

But some students, of all levels of ability, have great difficulty with phonics and word recognition. Generally, these students lag behind in reading although their language and cognitive development is average or higher. Their vocabulary and syntax are adequate (and often excellent) and their achievement in mathematics may be normal or superior. They have difficulty with the medium of reading—the print—and not usually with the message—the language and the ideas. Although they have good general ability and language comprehension, they tend to have difficulty with those aspects of reading related to learning the alphabetic principle. Even before reading is begun, during the preschool years, these students may have difficulty with phonemic awareness—rhyming and auditory sounding and blending—and with quickly naming objects and pictures. The younger children, especially, may have difficulty with discrimination of speech sounds.[1]

Children and adults who are later diagnosed with severe reading difficulty (learning disability, dyslexia) usually have had these problems with print and sounds during their early years and may still have them in the later grades and even as adults. It has been estimated that from ten to fifteen percent (recent estimates are higher) of the population has this problem and most are boys. Girls, as a group, are usually better at learning phonics than boys, and this is probably one of the reasons why girls, on the average, are better readers in the early grades than boys.

Why some people of normal and higher intelligence have difficulty with reading has been the subject of considerable research. Over the past century, psychologists, neurologists, psychiatrists, and educators have proposed various reasons. Some focused on poor teaching, while others sought answers in the social, psychological, and medical areas. The prevailing views on causation include neurological explanations (that reading disability stems from differences in the brain), educational explanations (that reading failure is caused by inadequate reading instructional methods), and social and emotional explanations (that reading problems come from the individual's social background and/or emotional problems). Increasingly, from about the 1960s, reading difficulties have been viewed by many as stemming from neurological factors, but one or more of the above causes may help explain an individual's reading problem; therefore, those with severe problems in learning to read should be referred for a comprehensive diagnosis.[2]

In the early grades reading comprehension usually suffers when students have difficulty with phonics and word recognition. During pre-adolescence and adulthood, many who had early reading problems also have difficulties with reading comprehension because they have not read enough to acquire the extensive vocabulary needed for reading at the fourth grade level and higher.[3]

What Should Be Done for Children Who Have Difficulty?

Should Those with Reading Problems Be Taught Phonics?

Although reading difficulty may, for some students, have a neurological base, there is considerable evidence that such individuals can learn to read if they receive balanced instruction—a program that includes instruction in phonics as well as reading stories for meaning. Children with early difficulty in phonemic awareness can be taught to rhyme and blend either before they learn to read, or while they are learning to read. This kind of instruction has been shown to benefit their reading development.[4]

It is important for the teacher and parents to know that while these students may find learning phonics difficult, with proper instruction they can and do learn it. They may need some adjustments in the regular program—more time, support, and practice—to reach a level similar to that of the rest of their class. But it is important to know that they can and do learn phonics.

Chapter 7, Part 3 gives suggestions on how to teach phonics to those having difficulty learning from the regular phonics programs selected for the class.[5] In general, for first graders and older children reading at a beginning first grade level, the teacher should determine each student's best way of learning to recognize words—sight, spelling patterns, or a visual/motor/kinesthetic approach (see Chapter 7, Part 3). The method by which the student learns best should be used as a start.

Prerequisite Phonic Skills

If the student has difficulty learning phonics, we suggest that his or her ability with underlying skills be assessed: rhyming skills, hearing sounds in words, discriminating and identifying beginning and ending sounds in words, and auditory blending. Also to be assessed are letter naming and prerequisite visual skills such as discriminating letters and letter sequences. These skills, called phonemic awareness, may need to be taught and practiced before phonics can be used effectively for word recognition.

Generally, weaknesses do not remain weaknesses forever. With practice and time, students who are given ample support are able to do what they could not do earlier. See Chapter 7, Part 3, pages 90 to 93 for suggestions on assessing prerequisite phonic skills.

Spelling Patterns and Phonic Blending

Once most of the prerequisite phonic skills are acquired and the student has learned some whole words, some consonant letter-sound correspondences can be taught. Then, a *spelling pattern approach* might be tried. It is usually easier to learn than a phonic-blending approach. In the spelling pattern approach the student is shown how to build words by changing the beginning consonant. Words the student knows as sight words can be used to identify other words by substituting the initial consonants known by the student (see Chapter 2, page 14, and Chapter 7, Part 2, page 73).

In a *phonic blending approach* the student who has learned to associate the letters with their sounds blends these to make words: /m/ /a/ /t/ to *mat* or /f/ /u/ /n/ to *fun*. This approach is more difficult for most students than a spelling pattern approach. The phonic blending approach, however, ultimately has more power in word identification. Therefore, a spelling pattern approach is suggested as an introduction to the more difficult phonic blending, and not as an end unto itself. Chapter 7, Part 3 gives suggestions for teaching both the spelling pattern and phonic blending approaches.

Students Who Overuse Phonics

Some students may overuse phonics—they continue to read by sounding out even those words that they know quite well. They seem to have no confidence in recognizing or identifying words without sounding and blending them. This may present a problem. But, on the positive side, it indicates that the phonic elements have been learned and are being applied, even if too diligently. A way to get students to stop this excessive sounding out is to have them read connected text orally, at a lively pace. You might take turns reading with them (one paragraph each) to pull the students along and to encourage taking chances with unfamiliar words. Reading aloud together or taking turns can be done with the teacher, a partner, or a group of students. Practice in reading along with audiotapes also helps, as does rereading the same book several times. In addition, the student should be encouraged to read books independently that are interesting and not too difficult.

Some people think that an overuse of phonics means that the student should not have been taught phonics to begin with. While this may appear to be so, in reality, students without phonic knowledge would probably be worse off as they continue to guess and misread words. For some children, oversounding is a phase in the development of reading skill, and they need only be helped to get beyond it.

A similar problem may exist in spelling, where some students may also overuse phonics. Their spelling is readable, but the most common words are often not spelled conventionally. Such students need to pay more attention to a word's appearance as well as its sound. This may be helped by practice in copying words, tracing words, and writing words to dictation from a partner who provides immediate feedback. Frequently used words and phrases are most appropriate for this. Use of the consonant substitution strategy discussed for reading can also be used in spelling (see Chapter 2, page 14).

The generalizations about sounding and spelling, and the skill in using these generalizations, are important for everyone to learn, especially for those who initially have difficulty learning to read.

Notes

1. Steven A. Stahl and Bruce A. Murray, "Defining Phonological Awareness and Its Relationship to Early Reading," *Journal of Educational Psychology,* 86 (1994): 221–231; Louise Spear-Swerling and Robert J. Sternbery *Off Track: When poor readers become "learning disabled"* (Boulder, CO: Westview Press, 1996).

2. Jeanne S. Chall and Rita W. Peterson, "The Influence of Neuroscience upon Educational Practice." In S. L. Friedman, K. A. Klivington, and R. W. Peterson (eds.), *The Brain, Cognition and Education* (Orlando, FL: Academic Press, 1986).

3. Jeanne S. Chall, Vicki A. Jacobs, and Luke E. Baldwin, *The Reading Crisis: Why Poor Children Fall Behind* (Cambridge: Harvard University Press, 1990).

4. Marilyn J. Adams, *Beginning to Read: Thinking and Learning about Print* (Cambridge: MIT Press, 1990).

5. Florence G. Roswell and Jeanne S. Chall, *Creating Successful Readers: A Practical Guide to Testing and Teaching at All Levels* (Chicago: Riverside Press, 1994).

6 The Place of Phonics in the Total Reading Program

Language, Cognition, and Word Identification

Phonics and other word identification skills should comprise only a part of the total reading program—a much larger part for beginners than for more advanced readers. One way to keep this in mind is to view reading itself as composed of three interrelated major components: language, cognition, and word identification.[1]

Before students learn to read, their language and cognitive abilities are considerable. Six-year-olds have speaking and listening vocabularies of 6,000 or more words, and they can understand, when heard, books that are far more advanced than they can read. At the beginning reading stage, decoding written words to their spoken counterparts usually leads directly to comprehension; most of the words in the selections are in their speaking and listening vocabularies, the syntax is within their language development, and the message of the paragraph or story is usually not beyond their cognitive abilities. Phonics is one of the techniques taught to enable beginning students to read the language they already use and understand.

Word recognition based on visual or picture clues and context also helps. Instruction in phonics, however, gives students a more powerful tool for identifying words—one that is more reliable than other word recognition techniques. Thus, phonics plays a major role in the reading program for the beginning reader.

Phonic instruction, to be effective, must provide the skills that can be applied to reading and writing stories and other selections. Since phonics is a tool for unlocking word pronunciation and for spelling words, its true value is realized only when applied to reading and writing, even at the earliest stage.

The focus on phonics and word recognition—with accuracy, speed, and confidence—should enable students to read independently and with understanding, as early as possible, books that are interesting and informative. When the basic phonic skills and rules are mastered, they can be used in an almost unconscious way. Students can also write words that can be identified by others, although the spelling may not always be correct.

As their word identification abilities begin to match their language and cognitive abilities, students can read materials of increasing difficulty. At more advanced reading levels, a good vocabulary and expanding general knowledge help the student further in identifying words automatically. Throughout, one needs to balance teaching and learning phonics with reading a variety of increasingly difficult texts. Such reading is necessary to expose students to words that are not identified immediately.

A caution—phonics teaching may also be overdone. It is easy to teach more letter-sound correspondences and phonic generalizations than are productive. A balance is necessary. Similarly, a program of book reading that excludes any phonic instruction may be equally weak by denying students an opportunity to gain the phonic knowledge necessary for identifying unknown or unfamiliar words. Most students will profit from a program that includes phonic instruction, word recognition practice, teacher guided oral and silent reading, independent reading and discussion of literature, creative writing, and spelling.

Phonics and Whole Language Programs

A whole language approach to reading instruction views reading development as occurring in a natural environment where learning to speak, read, listen, and write is coordinated. It tends to view learning to read as a natural process—one that is similar to learning to talk. The focus is on meaning and, for beginners, whole language teachers tend to favor books where the words are predictable and have rich context. Although phonics is not rejected, it is not generally taught systematically because it is assumed that phonics is best learned by reading books and environmental print (such as street signs and billboards). The position taken by most whole language proponents is that phonics should be learned incidentally and "as needed." Indeed, many whole language proponents have tended to think that if phonics is taught out of the context of stories, it will deter the development of meaningful reading.[2]

There is, however, a growing recognition and appreciation by many whole language advocates that young children develop phonemic awareness early. This awareness, they find, enhances the learner's ability to write, spell, and read.[3] Hence, instructional techniques that enhance phonemic awareness are being incorporated into whole language programs.

The focus is somewhat different in writing. Indeed, it has been thought for some time that a child's use of invented spelling leads to the natural discovery of sound-letter relations. When teachers write the conventional spelling for a child's invented spelling, they are reinforcing the idea that letters correspond to sounds and that they are rule governed. Calling attention to specific sound-letter correspondences will make this learning more explicit. The knowledge and skill students gain from such instruction provides a bridge to more mature reading and writing and to reading more difficult texts.

We believe that a structured phonics program, using the components described in the preceding sections, can fit into a whole language program. If a teacher chooses, however, to restrict phonics teaching to a more "on demand" approach, its effectiveness will depend greatly on his or her knowledge of phonics, skilled use of that knowledge, and sensitivity to the children's successes and failures. Teachers are always a strong determinant in children's learning. Indeed, the more flexible and open the methods used, the more influential the teacher becomes. Thus, particularly in a whole language classroom using incidental phonics instruction, it is essential that teachers are highly knowledgeable and skillful with regard to phonics and how it fits into student reading.

A procedure for incorporating phonics in whole language programs is outlined by Phyllis Trachtenburg.[4] For instance, she suggests teaching /ă/ (short a) to children who need it after reading a particular book. The teacher explains that the students are to learn a sound that the letter [a] stands for. She then prints a sample of the text from that book which gives many examples of the [a] to /ă/ correspondence and proceeds to teach it: underlining the letter, giving the sound in isolation and in the words; having the students listen for /ă/ and then having them repeat that sound in isolation and in words in the story; suggesting helpful cues such as "/ă/ as in apple"; guiding student practice in creating words with medial /ă/ in phonograms such as *at, an, am;* and building sentences using adjectives containing /ă/ and sentence clauses. Then the teacher presents a new book that contains many examples of /ă/ in the context and supports student participation in reading it.

Many of the suggestions for teaching phonics found in Part 2 of Chapter 7 may also be adapted for whole language classrooms.

The Relationship Between Writing/Spelling and Phonics

Much of the recent research on early reading has found that interest in writing appears to precede interest in reading. Dolores Durkin, in her study of children who learned to read before they entered school, found that a high proportion of these children showed interest not only in books and being read to, but in the letters, printed words, and writing.[5] She called them "paper-and-pencil kids." Earlier, Millie Almy also found that those first graders who made good progress in reading were interested in letters and print as well as in being read to.[6]

More recently, Glenda Bissex, in her study of the writing and reading development of her son when he was five to ten years of age, found that his early writing helped him gain insight into decoding and encoding (writing) words.[7] This was also the conclusion reached by Charles Read and Carol Chomsky.[8] With this knowledge, children have been observed to sound out the words they wish to write. As they try different letters to represent the sounds of these words, they become more aware that the letters represent sounds, and gain insight into the alphabetic principle. Their spelling is not conventional, as they often use the names of letters to replicate sounds in words rather than the sounds the letters represent. In spite of these differences, the practice of writing and sounding is excellent preparation for learning conventional spelling and phonics.

Invented spelling studies reinforce the recommendation to teach the names of the letters early. Knowledge of letter names will also help teachers and children communicate about reading and spelling. Once all the letters are learned, the children should be encouraged to write words as they hear them, and later as they are spelled conventionally. Indeed, in the Bissex study, her son sought conventional spellings in first grade, after using invented spellings in kindergarten, as have children in other studies. Early facility with writing contributes to the ease with which children learn conventional phonics and spelling.

Early writing also illustrates an important principle of learning and teaching: that learning is cumulative. Without knowing the alphabet letters and their names, children could not spontaneously use them in writing and invented spelling. Nor could they take up writing without developing auditory and visual discrimination skills.

During the earliest years, various language activities are important for the development of reading skills. Reading nursery rhymes to children, which serves to share our literary heritage, is also useful in developing their sensitivity to rhymes and the segmentation of words. Thus, we must look not only to the teaching and learning of the finished products—writing and reading comprehension—but to the prior learning on which they are based.

For spelling instruction, words can be dictated that use the letter-sound correspondences previously taught to make students more conscious of the separate letters and of the fact that just one different letter (or sound) at the beginning, middle, or end of a word makes a different word. It is also useful to dictate words that are not known, but whose spelling can be reasoned by analogy. Thus, if the students have practiced reading *cat, bat,* and *sat,* the teacher can dictate new words such as *fat, hat, mat, pat,* and *rat,* or even less familiar or nonsense words, such as *gat, tat, zat,* and *vat.*

Achievement in spelling and phonics is closely associated in the early grades. Those children who are good in phonics are usually good in spelling. And those who are good in phonics and spelling are usually good in word recognition, oral reading accuracy, and silent reading comprehension.

Why Do Some Phonics Programs Fail?

A phonics program may fail to give students the skills necessary to become good readers if those skills are insufficiently practiced, and if phonics is not adequately balanced with reading of texts. Teachers should not forget that the purpose of learning phonics is to help in the accurate and efficient identification of words when reading for comprehension.

A phonics program may also fail if it tries to teach too many elements and rules, no matter how useful they may be. Similarly, if knowledge gained in the phonics program is applied too strictly, as if it were the true and best way to identify every word, the program may fall short of expectation.

Notes

1. John B. Carroll, "Developmental Parameters of Reading Comprehension." In J. T. Guthrie (ed.) *Cognition, Curriculum and Comprehension,* (Newark, DE: International Reading Association, 1977).

2. Marie Carbo, "Debunking the Great Phonics Myth," *Phi Delta Kappan,* (November 1988): 226–40; Kenneth Goodman, *What's Whole in Whole Language?* (Portsmouth, NH: Heinemann, 1986).

3. Keith E. Stanovich, "Romance and Reason," *The Reading Teacher 47* (1994): 280–291.

4. Phyllis Trachtenburg, "Using Children's Literature to Enhance Phonics Instruction," *The Reading Teacher* (1990: 648–654).

5. Dolores Durkin, "Early Readers—Reflections after Six Years of Research," *The Reading Teacher* 18 (1964): 3–7.

6. Millie C. Almy, *Children's Experiences Prior to First Grade and Success in Beginning Reading* (New York: Columbia University Teachers College, 1949).

7. Glenda Bissex, *GNYS AT WRK: A Child Learns to Write and Read* (Cambridge: Harvard University Press, 1980).

8. Charles Read, "Preschool Children's Knowledge of English Phonology," *Harvard Educational Review,* 41, (1971): 1–34; Carol Chomsky, "Invented Spelling in the Open Classroom," in Walburga von Raffler-Engel (guest ed.), *Child Language—1975* (New York: International Linguistics Association, 1976).

7 Resources

1. PHONIC ELEMENTS AND GENERALIZATIONS IN ORDER OF SUGGESTED TEACHING

Some continuing questions in the teaching of phonics are, "How much do students need to learn, and in what order?" We present in this section the basic phonic elements and generalizations that students need to know and in the order that is generally most helpful.* These are in boxes for easy identification. In addition, we present phonic elements that occur less frequently and generalizations that are more advanced. These are unboxed and are presented for teachers who may wish to discuss them with students who are curious about letter-to-sound correspondences. We have found that the more students know, the more interesting phonics becomes.

It is not necessary to be strict about the order of teaching and learning phonic elements; it should be thought of in general terms:

- consonants precede vowels,
- short vowels precede long vowels in words with a final silent [e],
- long vowels with silent [e] precede vowel combinations,
- syllabication usually follows vowel combinations.

*These phonic elements and generalizations are based on analyses of the classic reading textbooks in American education and more recent phonological research by linguists on the nature of the English language (see Chapter 2). For prerequisite (prereading) skills usually taught in kindergarten, see Chapter 2, page 11.

J. P. Ives, L. Z. Bursuk, and S. A. Ives, *Word Identification Techniques* (Chicago: Rand McNally, 1979) was used as a general reference for this section. For those who want to delve deeper into these associations, we refer you to Richard Venezky, "English Orthography: Its Graphical Structure and Its Relation to Sound," *Reading Research Quarterly* 2 (1967): 75–105.

Throughout, [brackets] are used to indicate letters, /slash marks/ to indicate sounds, and *italics* for words.

Remember also, that students learn some phonic elements through reading connected text and do not need direct instruction in them. Calling them to students' attention may be all that is necessary. Generally, it is important not to overdo phonic instruction and to know that phonics and reading go together—that one supports the other.

Each of the phonic elements and generalizations is followed by illustrative words (see lists in the Appendix for additional words).

Consonants

Letter	Sound	Words	
		Initial	*Final*
[s]	/s/	*s*at, *s*it	bu*s*, ga*s*
[m]	/m/	*m*at, *m*iss	hi*m*, ha*m*
[t]	/t/	*t*am, *t*in	ha*t*, i*t*
[f]	/f/	*f*at, *f*it	i*f*, el*f*
[b]	/b/	*b*at, *b*it	ca*b*, fi*b*
[r]	/r/	*r*an, *r*ib	fa*r*, si*r*
[n]	/n/	*n*ot, *n*ame	ca*n*, ti*n*
[p]	/p/	*p*et, *p*ast	ca*p*, hi*p*
[d]	/d/	*d*esk, *d*og	ha*d*, hea*d*
[h]	/h/	*h*and, *h*at	—
[c]	/k/	*c*at, *c*ost	toni*c*, lila*c*
[g]	/g/	*g*ame, *g*ot	ta*g*, bi*g*
[j]	/j/	*j*et, *j*am	—
[l]	/l/	*l*et, *l*ost	pa*l*, goa*l*
[k]	/k/	*k*id, *k*ey	soa*k*, pee*k*
[v]	/v/	*v*an, *v*et	ga*v*e, ha*v*e
[w]	/w/	*w*et, *w*ill	—
[z]	/z/	*z*oo, *z*ebra	qui*z*, whi*z*
[qu]	/kw/	*qu*iz, *qu*ick	—
[y]	/y/	*y*ell, *y*es	—
[c]	/s/	*c*ent, *c*ity	fa*c*e, mi*c*e
[g]	/j/	*g*em, *g*ym	ca*g*e, hu*g*e
[x]	/ks/		bo*x*, mi*x*
[s]	/z/		hi*s*, bear*s*
[s]	/sh/	*s*ure, *s*ugar	

[v] is almost always followed by [e] in final position
[y] functions as a vowel in final position (*very, merry*)
plural [s] = /z/ after voiced consonants (*dogs, beds*)
[s] = /sh/ in *sure* and *sugar* only

The consonant letter-sound correspondences are listed above in an order suggested for teaching based on their frequency, discriminability (both auditory and visual), ease of learning, and usefulness in producing words when combined with single vowel letters. The continuants (consonant sounds that may be prolonged) are listed first because they are most easily separated from the other sounds of a word. The first six consonants listed above may be combined with the short vowel sounds of [a] and [i] to form a reasonable set of words for initial instruction.

The letters [c] and [g] each represent two sounds—one "hard" and the other "soft."

The hard [c] is the sound of /k/ as in *cat*. The soft sound represented by [c] is /s/ as in *cent, center,* and *city*.
When [c] is followed by [e], [i], or [y], the sound is usually soft.

The hard [g] is the sound of /g/ as in *game*. The soft sound of [g] is /j/ as in *gem* and *gentle*.
When [g] is followed by [e], [i], or [y], the sound is usually soft.

Note that for some easy, common words this does not hold true: *get, gift, girl, give*.

A final [e] may signal [c] = /s/ as well as marking the preceding vowel as long (*grace, mice*).

"Short" Vowels

We suggest teaching short vowels first because they are more frequent in the English language than the long vowels and combinations. The first two vowels suggested for teaching, [a] and [i], with their corresponding short sounds, are easily discriminable and yield many CVC (consonant-vowel-consonant) words for teaching, e.g., *bat, ran.*

Short vowel rule: When a short word (or syllable) with one vowel letter ends in a consonant, the vowel sound is usually short.

Letter	Sound	Words	
		Initial	*Medial*
[a]	/ă/	*at, an*	*cat, can*
[i]	/ĭ/	*it, in*	*hit, tin*
[e]	/ĕ/	*egg, end*	*leg, met*
[o]	/ŏ/	*on, ox*	*hot, hog*
[u]	/ŭ/	*up, us*	*cup, bug*

Word patterns that follow this generalization are as follows:

VC	CVC	CVCC	CCVC
am	*ham*	*damp*	*stem*

These patterns also occur in stressed syllables of polysyllabic words, as in *ham'·ster.*

The vowel letter-sound correspondences are more difficult to learn than the consonants because each vowel letter represents more than one sound and the sounds are harder to discriminate. The most common vowels are the short sounds: (/ă/ as in *apple*, /ĕ/ as in *egg*, /ĭ/ as in *Indian*, /ŏ/ as in *octopus*, and /ŭ/ as in *umbrella*).

Consonant Blends

> Two or more consonant letters may stand for a blend, e.g., <u>bl</u>ock, <u>cr</u>ib, <u>spl</u>it.

Initial consonant blends with [l]

Letters	Sound	Words
[bl]	/bl/	*blend, black*
[cl]	/kl/	*clock, clip*
[fl]	/fl/	*flat, flag*
[gl]	/gl/	*glad, glass*
[pl]	/pl/	*plug, plank*
[sl]	/sl/	*sled, slam*

Initial consonant blends with [r]

Letters	Sound	Words
[br]	/br/	*brat, brass*
[cr]	/kr/	*crib, crab*
[dr]	/dr/	*dress, draft*
[gr]	/gr/	*grill, grass*
[fr]	/fr/	*fresh, frog*
[pr]	/pr/	*prank, press*
[tr]	/tr/	*trip, track*

Initial consonant blends beginning with [s]

Letters	Sound	Words
[sc]	/sk/	*scat, scan*
[sk]	/sk/	*skip, skin*
[sm]	/sm/	*small, smoke*
[sn]	/sn/	*snip, snap*
[sp]	/sp/	*spin, spill*
[st]	/st/	*step, still*
[sw]	/sw/	*swap, swim*
[sl]	/sl/	*slap, slip*

Initial three-letter consonant blends

Letters	Sound	Words
[scr]	/skr/	*scrap, scratch*
[spl]	/spl/	*splash, split*
[spr]	/spr/	*spring, sprig*
[str]	/str/	*string, strut*

No new associations have to be learned for the consonant blends. The students need only be made aware of blending together two or three consonant sounds that they have learned already; e.g., /st/ for [st] in *stop,* /spr/ for [spr] in *spring.* Most students will have learned some blends while reading stories and other text. The advantage of calling attention to them is that they can then be recognized as units when decoding unfamiliar words.

Consonant Blends (cont.)

Other common blends are grouped below acording to whether they occur in the initial or final position of a word.*

Initial Consonant Blends			Final Consonant Blends		
Letters	Sound	Words	Letters	Sound	Words
[dw]	/dw/	dwarf	[ct]	/kt/	pact
[qu]	/kw/	quick	[ft]	/ft/	left
[scr]	/skr/	scream	[ld]	/ld/	fold
[spr]	/spr/	spring	[lf]	/lf/	self
[str]	/str/	strike	[lk]	/lk/	bulk
[tw]	/tw/	twin	[lt]	/lt/	halt
			[mp]	/mp/	lamp
			[nd]	/nd/	and
			[nk]	/nk/	bank
			[nt]	/nt/	ant
			[rb]	/rb/	herb
			[rd]	/rd/	hard
			[rk]	/rk/	hark
			[rl]	/rl/	hurl
			[rm]	/rm/	harm
			[rn]	/rn/	barn
			[rp]	/rp/	harp
			[rst]	/rst/	first
			[rt]	/rt/	hurt
			[sk]	/sk/	ask
			[sp]	/sp/	wasp
			[st]	/st/	fist

*A reminder: These, as with other unboxed elements, are for your information. It is not necessary to make them part of the curriculum.

Final Geminate (Double) Consonants and [ck]

> At the end of some words, and sometimes in the middle of
> two-syllable words, the same two letters are written for one
> sound, e.g., *still, mess, mutt, muffin, rabbit*. Similarly, the
> final /k/ sound is often written with the letters [ck].

Letters	Sound	Words	
		Medial	*Final*
[bb]	/b/	*rabbit*	*ebb*
[dd]	/d/	*middle*	*add*
[ff]	/f/	*muffin*	*cuff*
[ll]	/l/	*cellar*	*hill*
[pp]	/p/	*happy*	—
[ss]	/s/	*messy*	*miss*
[tt]	/t/	*flatten*	*mitt*
[ck]	/k/	*thicken*	*sock*

[ss] also stands for /sh/ as in *ti<u>ss</u>ue*

Again, most students will have met these combinations in context and acquired them without any effort. Simply calling attention
to them should make students more aware of them.

Consonant Digraphs

> Consonant digraphs are two consonant letters that together stand for a sound entirely different from either letter alone; e.g., [ch] stands for /ch/ in *chop,* [sh] for /sh/ in *shop.*

That two letters may stand for one sound is a new concept. Some students may be familiar with it because the digraphs occur in high frequency words such as *the, that, she, shall.*

Letter	Sound	Words	
		Initial	*Final*
[ch]	/ch/	*chop, chin*	*such, much*
[ph]	/f/	*phone, phase*	*graph, humph*
[sh]	/sh/	*ship, shot*	*cash, dish*
[th]	/th/	*think, thin*	*path, with*
[th]	/TH/	*then, that*	*bathe, clothe* (usually followed by [e] in final position)
[wh]*	/hw/	*whip, when*	—
[tch]	/ch/	—	*hatch, pitch* (final position only)
[ch]	/sh/	*chalet, chef*	
[ch]	/k/	*character, chorus*	
[gh]	/f/	—	*rough* (final position only)
[ng]	/ŋ/	—	*ring* (final position only)

The letters [gh] represent /f/ in only a few words, but some of these are very common words, such as *cough, laugh, enough.*

The consonant combination of [tch], which is a digraph plus a silent letter, is usually taught with the digraphs because it represents the same sound as [ch].

Note that the two sounds represented by [th], voiced and voiceless, are listed separately above although we do not recommend teaching them separately. Even accomplished readers are apt to be unaware of the voiced and voiceless sounds of [th]. Most words that

*[wh] is listed even though it does not strictly fit the definition of a consonant digraph (i.e., the sound it represents, /hw/, is not *different* from either of the letters in the digraph, but the sounds are reversed).

have a voiced [th] (shown as /TH/ above) in initial position are function words—that is, words like *this, that, the, them, those, than, their, these, then.* The shift from voiceless [th] (as in *thing*) to voiced in the function words will come quite naturally, especially for native English-language speakers.

Consonant Digraph Blends

Sometimes a consonant digraph is followed (or preceded) by another consonant; e.g., *shrill, parch*. These consonant sequences are called consonant digraph blends, and students who have learned the consonant digraphs usually easily decode these in context. We do not recommend teaching them.

Initial consonant digraph blends

Letters	Sound	Words
*[chl]	/kl/	*chlorine*
[chr]	/kr/	*chrome*
*[phl]	/fl/	*phlegm*
*[phr]	/fr/	*phrase*
[shr]	/shr/	*shrink*
*[sph]	/sf/	*sphere*
[thr]	/thr/	*three*
*[thw]	/thw/	*thwack*

Final consonant digraph blends

Letters	Sound	Words
*[dth]	/dth/	*width*
*[fth]	/fth/	*fifth*
*[lch]	/lch/	*filch*
*[lfth]	/lfth/	*twelfth*
*[lph]	/lf/	*sylph*
*[lsh]	/lsh/	*Welsh*
*[lth]	/lth/	*wealth*
*[mph]	/mf/	*lymph*
[nch]	/nch/	*bench*
*[ngth]	/ŋkth/	*length*
[nth]	/nth/	*tenth*
[rch]	/rch/	*birch*
*[rmth]	/rmth/	*warmth*
*[rsh]	/rsh/	*harsh*
[rth]	/rth/	*forth*

*These are infrequent combinations, but may be found in very common words.

"Long" Vowels with Final [e]

Since the long vowel sounds are the same as the letter names, these are easier to learn. Introduction to long vowels is usually through the "magic [e] rule," the consonant + vowel + consonant + [e] (CVCe) spelling pattern (*fame, time, home, mule*).

Magic [e] rule: When a short word ends with an [e], the first vowel usually has the long sound and the final [e] is silent.

Letter	Sound	Words
[a]	/ā/	*make, made*
[e]	/ē/	*these, Pete*
[i]	/ī/	*bike, line*
[o]	/ō/	*pole, cone*
[u]	/yü/	*mule, cute*
[u]	/ü/	*rule, prune*

Word or syllable patterns that follow this generalization are as follows:

VCe	CVCe	CCVCe
ape	*cape*	*brave*

The first step in teaching is to pair contrasting CVC and CVCe words such as *mad-made, fat-fate, hat-hate, bit-bite, kit-kite, rob-robe*. Students should say the pair and observe the difference between the words.

When teaching the [uCe] pattern, it is usually less confusing to present only long [u], i.e., /yü/ as in *cute*, even though [uCe] is often decoded as /ü/ as in *rule*. Most readers easily adjust to the slight change in sound. The reader should try long [u], i.e., /yü/, and if the result is not a word, the adjustment to /ü/ is almost spontaneous, as in *rule, June, Duke, flute, dune*.

The more technical magic [e] rule is: When a word has a single vowel letter followed by a single consonant*, followed by a final [e], the single vowel letter represents the long vowel and the final [e] is silent.

---

*Be aware that "single consonant" here refers to the sound. Therefore, when two consonants representing one sound are followed by the "magic [e]," the vowel is long, e.g., [th] followed by [e] as in *clothe, bathe*.

"Long" Vowels with Final [e] (cont.)

Words Ending in [ve]

Words ending in [ve] often do not follow the "magic [e]"rule because, in English orthography, [v] is hardly ever found in final position (*have, love, live*).

Other Exceptions

In words ending in the letters [dge], the final [e] is there to <u>signal</u> that the [g] represents its soft sound (*nudge, edge*). It does not signal a preceding long vowel.

"Long" Vowels at the End of Words or Syllables

> When a word or a syllable has only one vowel and it comes at the end of the word or syllable, it usually stands for the long sound.

Letter	Sound	Words
[a]	/ā/	*na·tion, pa·tient*
[e]	/ē/	*she, me, he·ro*
[i]	/ī/	*pi·lot, mi·nor*
[o]	/ō/	*go, no, mo·ment*
[u]	/yü/ or	*mu·sic, hu·man*
[u]	/ü/	*du·ty*

Word patterns that follow this generalization are as follows:

CV   CV·CVC

he   *ti·ger*

[y] as a Vowel

[y] at the end of a word is a vowel.

When [y] follows a consonant at the end of words of more than one syllable, it stands for the long sound of [e].

Letter	Sound	Words
[y]	/ē/	*fluffy, puppy, kitty, pretty*

When [y] follows a consonant at the end of one-syllable words, it usually stands for the long sound of [i].

Letter	Sound	Words
[y]	/ī/	*fry, my, spy, cry*

Vowels Followed by [r]

> When a vowel letter is followed by [r], the vowel sound is different from either the long or short vowel sound.

Letter	Sound	Words
[ar]	/ä(r)/	ark, car, hard, part·ner
[or]	/ô(r)/	cork, cord, fort, form·er
[er]	/ə(r)/	her, fern, germ, ger·bil
[ir]	/ə(r)/	bird, first, sir, dir·ty
[ur]	/ə(r)/	hurt, burst, nurse, fur·nish

Note that [er], [ir], [ur] (and [yr]) stand for the same sound.

[yr] /ə(r)/   mar·tyr

Word or syllable patterns that follow this generalization are as follows:

V[r]	CV[r]	CV[r]C
or	for	form

Silent Consonants

> Two consonant letters may represent the sound of only one of them. The other consonant is "silent." These combinations usually occur in either initial or final position.

Letters	Sound	Words	
		Initial	*Final*
[ck]	/k/	—	*back, stick*
[dge]	/j/	—	*dodge, hedge*
[gh]	/g/	*ghost, ghastly*	—
[gn]	/n/	*gnaw, gnat*	*sign, foreign*
[lk]	/k/	—	*walk, talk*
[kn]	/n/	*know, knee*	—
[mb]	/m/	*limb, lamb*	—
[sc]	/s/	*scene, scent*	—
[wr]	/r/	*wring, wreck*	—

Usually, only the above consonant combinations with a silent consonant are taught, but students will come across others listed below and may inquire about them. In the past, many of these letters were sounded separately. In Middle English, for instance, *gnash* and *gnat* were pronounced /gnash/ and /gnat/—with both the [g] and the [n] sounds.

Less Common Initial Silent Consonants

Letters	Sound	Words
[mn]	/n/	*mnemonic*
[pn]	/n/	*pneumonia*
[pt]	/t/	*ptomaine*
[rh]	/r/	*rhyme*
[sw]	/s/	*sword*
[wh]	/h/	*who, whole* (largely represented by a few very frequent words)

Less Common Final Silent Consonants

Letters	Sound	Words
[bt]	/t/	*doubt*
[gn]	/n/	*sign*
[ld]	/d/	*could, should, would* (in these words only)
[lf]	/f/	*half*
[lm]	/m/	*calm*

Word Analysis: Noun Inflections—Plurals

> **[s] and [es] signify plurals.**

This concept is easily acquired. The [s] may stand for /s/ as in *cats* or for /z/ as in *dogs*. The [es] stands for /ez/ as in *foxes*. These distinctions come naturally since they have been acquired while learning the language; they need not be taught. You may, however, wish to inform an inquisitive student that the plural [s] sometimes stands for /s/ and sometimes /z/.

Word Analysis: Verb Inflections—[ed], [ing], [s]

> The inflectional endings [s], [ed], and [ing] are additions to base words that make the word "fit" the meaning of the sentence; i.e., make it grammatically correct.

Ending	Purpose	Examples
[ed]	signals the past tense of a verb	he *hopped*, she *played*
[ing]	signals the present participle of verbs	he is *hopping*, she is *playing*
[s], [es]	used for third person singular verbs	he *hops*, she *plays*, it *buzzes*, she *mixes*

As with plurals, verb inflections come naturally as a function of knowing the language. It is not necessary, therefore, to point out the different sounds represented by [ed]; i.e., /d/ as in *pulled,* /t/ as in *tapped,* and sometimes /ed/ as in *landed.* When the inflectional ending [ed] is added to a verb base ending with /t/ or /d/, the result is a syllable pronounced /ed/ as in *waited, faded.* When [ed] is added to a base ending with any voiceless consonant except /t/ (that is, /p/, /k/, /f/, or /s/), it is pronounced /t/ as in *trapped, packed.* In all other cases, when [ed] is added to a base, it is pronounced /d/ as in *cried, plugged.*

The verb endings [s], [ed], and [ing], as with other inflections, change a word form to one with a new grammatical or syntactic relationship. Recognizing these endings gives students a word identification technique as well as signaling meaning.

Vowel Digraphs

> When a word or syllable has a vowel digraph (two vowels together), the first vowel usually stands for the long sound and the second vowel is silent.

Letter	Sound	Words
[ai]	/ā/	*paid, pail*
[ay]	/ā/	*pay, day*
[oa]	/ō/	*boat, goal*
[ee]	/ē/	*tree, beet*
[ea]*	/ē/	*meal, steam*

*[ea] also often represents /ĕ/ as in *bread, head*

The vowel digraphs presented here are frequent in the language and easy to learn. While the generalization does not operate one hundred percent of the time, it does fit many common words. Other vowel digraphs and diphthongs will be found on pages 61–62.

Syllabication

There are visual cues that can be used to help readers syllabicate (break down) an unrecognized long word. Once a long word has thus been broken down into smaller parts, those parts can be decoded according to the phonic generalizations learned, and then blended together to form the whole word.*

Introduce syllabication by dividing short compound words between the two words. (See the list, page 140, of two-syllable compound words.) Students should understand that a syllable must have a vowel sound. Where a word is divided will suggest whether to try the long or short sound of the vowel. Vowel digraphs ([ea], [ai], [oa], etc.), consonant digraphs ([ch], [sh], [th], etc.), and consonant blends ([tr], [cr], [bl], etc.) usually remain in one syllable and keep their sound.

The guidelines presented below are for reading, not for syllabicating words in writing. The first three can be taught early, after long vowels in words ending with [e]; i.e., the [CVCe] pattern. The remaining ones are more advanced and should be taught later.

Compound words
   Separate the two words already known if they appear together in a long word.
   pan·cake, pea·nut, tom·cat

Inflectional endings—[ing], [er], [est], [ed]
   The word endings [ing] (*swing·ing, mail·ing, bit·ing*); [er] (*work·er, small·er, strong·er*); [est] (*low·est, tall·est, long·est*); and sometimes [es] (*dress·es, box·es, pass·es*) and [ed] (*land·ed, plant·ed, point·ed*) often make up separate syllables.

---

*There are other strategies that have to do with whether a syllable is accented or not, but these are usually not helpful. If a word is not recognized, the reader is not likely to know which syllable is accented.

Two medial consonants: CVC·CVC Words
    When two or more consonant letters come together in the middle of a word, divide the word between the consonants. Then try the short sound for the vowel in the first syllable (*can·dy, den·tist, pic·nic, bon·net, but·ton*).

Exception: Keep [ch], [tch], [ck], [ph], [sh], and [th] together when you divide a word *(bush·el, fath·om, graph·ic, hatch·et, chick·en).*

Two-syllable words with one medial consonant
    When only one consonant comes between two vowels, divide the word before the consonant and try the long sound of the first vowel (*pi·lot, o·ver, pa·gan, e·vil, to·tal, na·sal, ma·son*). If the long sound doesn't make a word, divide the word after the consonant and try the short sound for the first vowel (*ex·it, ton·ic, pris·on, piv·ot, val·id, tim·id, sec·ond*).

Two-syllable words ending in a consonant plus [le]
    When a word ends in a consonant plus [le], divide it before that consonant. If the first syllable ends in a consonant, try the short sound of the vowel (*pud·dle, rid·dle, spin·dle, bun·dle, sin·gle, sam·ple, rip·ple*). If the first syllable ends with a vowel, try the long sound of the vowel (*ti·tle, ri·fle, bri·dle, o·gle, ti·tle, tri·fle*).

Two-syllable words ending in a consonant plus [re]
    When a two-syllable word ends in a consonant plus [re], divide it before that consonant. If the first syllable ends with a vowel, try the long sound of that vowel (*acre, metre, fibre, ogre*). Very infrequently (noticeably in British spellings), the first syllable ends in a consonant, in which case, try the short sound of the vowel (*lus·tre, cen·tre, spec·tre*).

<u>Two-syllable words with vowel digraphs and diphthongs</u>
Divide the word using syllabication strategies above and use the sounds you have learned for the digraphs: (1) between two medial consonants (*el·bow, cel·lar, pil·low, mil·dew, can·teen*); (2) before the single medial consonant (*de·tail, re·tail, i·deal, re·veal, o·cean, de·tain*) or, if that doesn't work; divide (3) after the single medial consonant (*shad·ow, wid·ow, sin·ew, trav·ail*).

Additional Word Analysis

The following word analysis concepts are useful in gaining meaning from the text and also for decoding.

Word Analysis: Contractions

> Contractions are shortened forms of words in which sounds or letters are deleted and an apostrophe replaces the letter(s) dropped.

Contraction	For	Words
[n't]	not	*can't, doesn't, didn't, haven't*
['ll]	will	*she'll, they'll, we'll, he'll*
['s]	is	*he's, she's, it's, what's,*
['re]	are	*you're, we're, they're*
['m]	am	*I'm*

Word Analysis: Possessives

['s] signals possession	[s'] signals plural possession
Bill's dog = dog belonging to Bill	the *girls'* home = home belonging to several girls
the *girl's* eyes = eyes belonging to the girl	the *birds'* cage = cage belonging to several birds

Word Analysis: Comparatives

[er]   the comparative form of adjectives and adverbs: *calmer, colder, hotter*
[est]   the superlative form of adjectives and adverbs: *calmest, coldest, hottest*

Variant Vowel Digraphs and Diphthongs

Students should learn that some vowel digraphs stand for more than one sound; e.g., [ou] in *soup* and *out,* and [ow]* in *how* and *crow*. They should also learn some of the exceptions to the generalization presented earlier, "When a word or syllable has two vowel letters together, the first vowel usually stands for the long sound and the second vowel is silent," especially the vowel digraphs that represent diphthongs; e.g., [oi] in *soil*, [oy] in *toy*, [ou] in *out*, and [ow] in *how*. The list given below includes vowel digraphs that stand for more than one sound, those that stand for diphthongs, and some that do both.

A **diphthong** is a blend of vowel sounds. Although some long vowel sounds are diphthongs (long [i] and [u]), it is common practice to use the term "diphthongs" to refer only to the following sounds: /oi/ (*boil*), /ou/ (*mouth*). It is not important to know which sounds are diphthongs, but it is important to teach the sounds represented by the digraphs that are boxed below. It is also important for students to be flexible.

When a word has one of the following vowel combinations, it usually represents the sounds indicated below.**

*The [w] serves as a vowel in some digraphs.
**When two sounds are given, the most frequent one is given first. Vowel digraph associations with a frequency of ten or less in the Hanna and Hodges study of 17,310 words are not listed. (Paul Hanna, Jean Hanna, Richard E. Hodges, Edwin H. Rudorf, Jr., *Phoneme-Grapheme Correspondences as Cues to Spelling Improvement*. Washington, D. C.: Office of Education, 1966.)

Variant Vowel Digraphs and Diphthongs (cont.)

Letters	Sound	Words
[ou]	/ou/	out, loud
	/ü/	soup, youth
[oo]	/ü/	pool, room
	/ù/	book, foot
[ow]	/ō/	crow, low
	/ou/	crown, down
[au]	/ô/	cause, haul
[aw]	/ô/	claw, lawn
[oi]	/oi/	moist, coin
[oy]	/oi/	boy, joy
[ew]	/yü/	few, new
	/ü/	drew, crew
[ie]	/ē/	piece, believe
	/ī/	pie, tie
[oe]	/ō/	toe, hoe

[ue]	/yü/	cue, value
[eu]	/yü/	feud, neutron
[ei]	/ā/	eight, rein
	/ē/	ceiling, protein
[ey]	/ē/	donkey (often shown as short [i] in dictionaries)
	/ā/	they, obey, grey

Prefixes and Suffixes

> Prefixes and suffixes are added to base words to make words with new meanings. A prefix is at the beginning of the word (pre·test); a suffix at the end of the word (care·<u>less</u>).

When students are decoding unknown multisyllabic words, it is to their advantage to know prefixes and suffixes. Such knowledge will also help in learning the meaning of the word.

Students should learn to recognize words with prefixes and suffixes and assign them their correct meanings. Some common prefixes and suffixes are listed below according to their frequency. Many have more meanings than the one given.

Prefix	Meaning	Example	Suffix	Meaning	Example
un	not or opposite of	*uneasy* *untie*	ful	full of	*spoonful*
re	again	*refile*	less	without	*hopeless*
dis	not or opposite of	*dishonest* *disappear*	ly	characteristic of	*quickly*
mis	wrongly	*misfire*	ness	state of, condition of	*sickness*
de	opposite of	*defrost*	able	can be done	*lovable*
en	cause to	*enable*	ible	can be done	*forcible*
fore	before	*foresight*	er	person connected with	*farmer*
im	not	*impossible*	or	person connected with	*debtor*
in	not	*inefficient*	ment	action or process	*government*
pre	before	*pre-war*	en	made of	*ashen*
bi	two	*bisect*	ion	act, process	*violation*
ex	former	*ex-wife*	ize	subject to, make	*humanize*
sub	under	*sub-basement*	ist	person who	*pianist*
mid	middle	*midbrain*	ity	state of	*musicality*
mal	poorly	*malpractice*	y	characterized by	*snowy*
trans	across	*transcontinental*	ous	possessing the qualities of	*murderous*
non	not	*nonsmoker*	let	small	*piglet*
pro	for	*pro-labor*	like	like	*homelike*
			ship	art, skill; state of being	*ownership*
			some	characterized by	*irksome*

Schwa

The "schwa" (sometimes called a "neutral" vowel or a "murmur" vowel) is an unstressed vowel sound such as the first sound in *around*, or the last vowel sound in *custom*. Any of the vowel letters may represent the schwa under specific circumstances. While some programs give generalizations on the schwa, we find them cumbersome and not very useful. For example, a generalization may first require the student to determine where the accent is. If the student knows that, he or she already knows the word. Words that contain the schwa may usually be decoded successfully if the reader tries the short sound of the vowel.

Vowel Letters [a] and [u] Followed by the Letter [l]

When [a], and sometimes [u], is followed by [l], often the vowel is neither short nor long (*ball, halt, pull*).

Letters	Sound	Words
[al]	/ ôl /	*fall, bald*
[ul]	/ ü /	*full, pulley*

Word or syllable patterns that follow this generalization are as follows:

C[al]	C[ul]	C[al]C
fall	*bull*	*scald*

Usually, this generalization is not taught because there are many common word exceptions (*pal, gal·lop, gull, dull*). Even though not taught, it is nevertheless helpful to explain to questioning students that [l] often does influence a preceding [a] or [u] resulting in exceptions to the short vowel rule.

Vowel Letters [a] and [o] Preceded by [w]

When the vowel letters [a] or [o] are preceded by [w] in a word or syllable, the sound of the vowel may be other than short or long.

Letters	Sound	Words
[wa]	/ wô /	*wand, wad, waddle*
[wo]	/ wü /	*wolf, woman*

Again, this generalization, even though not taught, is helpful in explaining why many common words, in which [w] is followed by [a] or [o], do not contain a short vowel sound.

Word Patterns

Students should be made aware of certain spelling patterns that represent sounds different from what might be expected. The ones listed below do not occur in many words, but the words have a high frequency and, therefore, students will come across them early in their reading. For this reason, you should call attention to the patterns.

<u>Vowel-consonant</u>

Pattern	Sound	Words
[ild]	/īld/	*child, mild, wild* (no others)
[ind]	/īnd/	*blind, mind, grind*
[igh]	/ī/	*high, sigh, thigh, nigh*
[ight]	/īt/	*right, might*
[old]	/ōld/	*old, bold, cold*
[olt]	/ōlt/	*bolt, colt, jolt*
[ost]	/ōst/	*ghost, host, most* (common exceptions are short [o] in *cost, frost, lost*)

Some teachers prefer to give generalizations for the long [i] and long [o] patterns. That is, **When [i] is the only vowel within a syllable and it is followed by [ld], [nd], or [gh], the vowel sound is long [i].** Similarly, **When [o] is the only vowel within a syllable and is followed by [ld], [lt], or [st], the vowel sound is long [o].** Our preference, however, is simply to make students aware of these vowel consonant patterns along with the others given above.

2. SUGGESTIONS FOR TEACHING CONCEPTS ABOUT PRINT, PHONEMIC AWARENESS, AND PHONIC ELEMENTS AND GENERALIZATIONS

General guidelines for teaching phonics are given in Chapter 4. In this section we offer some specific strategies for teaching some of the most essential concepts, phonic elements, and generalizations. Time spent actively teaching phonics to students gives teachers a sense of students' progress. It also contributes greatly to the students' learning and understanding of phonics. If done well and enthusiastically, it will impart to them the importance of learning phonics for achieving competence and independence in reading.

The teaching strategies in this section will be most effective if an attitude of inquiry, interest, and importance is maintained. Phonic lessons should usually be followed by reading sentences, stories, or books containing some of the elements learned.

The suggestions that follow do not exhaust the useful strategies for teaching phonics. Rather, they are suggestions for a lesson (or sometimes several lessons, each marked with a bullet) usually included in a complete phonics program.* They are included here as a resource for teachers. Indeed, we hope the suggested lessons will spark individual teachers' creativity and imagination. There are limitless ways to teach the concepts, elements, and phonic generalizations. Review is essential, and varied strategies for review are encouraged to maintain interest.

At the end of many lessons, a page reference is given for the appropriate word list in the Appendix that gives additional words for teaching the specific element or concept.

Print Concepts: Stories, Sentences, Words, Letters

- Use storybooks familiar to the children to talk about the concepts *stories, sentences, words,* and *letters.* Encourage students to use these words in their discussion.

- Print a sentence from a familiar book on the board and read it aloud. Tell the children, "This is a *sentence,*" and frame it with your hands. Point to each word as you read the sentence again and ask them what these (pointing to the words) are called.

*For the most part, lessons included in this section have been adapted from *Chall-Popp Phonics* (Elizabethtown, PA: Continental Press, 1996). See Chapter 3, particularly pages 18-19, for suggestions regarding when to teach the concepts, phonic elements, and generalizations.

Count the *words* with the children and have them tell you how many *words* there are in the sentence.

Circle a letter and establish that it is a *letter*, and that we use *letters* to write *words*.

Ask individual students to circle *words* on the board—the first, second, and third *word*, or the name of a person or other distinctive word. Ask students to copy some of the words. Reinforce the concept that they are using *letters* to write *words*. Repeat this activity and ask a student to take the role of teacher.

Print Concepts: The Alphabet, Capital Letters, and Lowercase Letters

- Have an alphabet chart (with capital and lowercase letters) or cards on display in the room and establish that the entire group of letters is called the *alphabet*. Have students repeat the word *alphabet* and tell something about it—what the first letter is, what we use it for, etc.
- Point out the two forms for each letter in the alphabet display. Indicate which are *capital* or *uppercase letters* and which are *small* or *lowercase letters*. Ask the children to repeat each phrase. Then point to a series of letters and ask children to tell you if each one is a *capital letter* or a *lowercase letter*. Have students take turns being teacher in this or similar activities.
- Ask the children to count aloud with you the letters in the alphabet and establish that there are 26 letters in our alphabet—26 capital letters or 26 lowercase letters. Students who can name the letters might be invited to join you in reciting them as you point to them in sequence.
- Teach the traditional alphabet song.

The Alphabet: Recognizing, Naming, and Writing

- Begin to teach the letters in alphabetic sequence. Work with recognizing, naming, and writing a small set of letters at a time.

Print a small set of capital letters (e.g., A, B, C, D, and E) in alphabetic sequence on the board and have the class say the names of the letters with you. Provide a strong leading voice. Individual students may read the letters as you point to them, first in sequence, and then randomly.

Then ask individuals to point to the letters on the board as you name them in random order. Be sure to ask for *capital A* or *lowercase a,* for example.

Provide opportunities for students to recognize these letters in the context of words and sentences in books.

Repeat the same procedure with the matching set of lowercase letters.

Repeat the procedure with small sets of the remaining capital and lowercase letters.

- When both capital and lowercase letters in the set have been taught, print the capital and lowercase letters in random order on the board. Ask the entire class, and then individuals, to read them aloud.

- Give students letter cards that they can hold up when you name specific letters, both in alphabetic sequence and in random order.

- Using very large hand and arm movements, print individual letters in the air (with your back to the children). Have children join you. Choose a student to be the teacher to continue the modeling while you move among the children, giving them guidance as needed.

- Print large letters on the board for students to trace over and finally to copy onto paper.

- For students having difficulty, print the letters lightly on paper for them to trace. Provide large letter cards for them to trace with their fingers.

- Print a phrase or a short sentence on the board in capital letters and ask students to print it on their papers using lowercase letters, and vice versa.

Phonemic Awareness: Rhyming

- Read Mother Goose rhymes and other poems and jingles to the class. Ask the children to repeat the rhymes with you and then to repeat the rhyming words. Ask them to think of other words that rhyme.

- Read rhymes, pausing just before the word that rhymes with the word in the preceding line. Ask students to fill in the missing rhyming word. For instance, wait for students to fill in the word *hill* as you read, "Jack and Jill, Went up the _____, To fetch a pail of water." Wait again for the word *crown*; "Jack fell down, And broke his _____, And Jill came tumbling after."

This activity can be started with very familiar rhymes and work up to less familiar ones. For the less familiar rhymes, encourage students to think of words that will rhyme and also fit the context.

- Encourage students to make up rhymes. They can begin by thinking of rhyming words (for example, *big* and *pig*) and then make up little jingles (for example, "My spotted pink *pig*, Grew very *big*").

Phonemic Awareness: Auditory Blending

- Begin auditory blending with compound words. Segment them and ask students to say the whole word. For instance, you might separate the two parts of these words by about half a second and ask students for the whole word:

home/made	snow/ball	foot/ball
sail/boat	out/side	post/man

(See page 140 for additional words.)

Then introduce the blending of initial consonant sounds by separating simple CVC words into two parts—between the initial consonant and the vowel-consonant ending. Pause about a half a second between saying the parts as illustrated below:

s/ad	m/en	t/an
r/ed	f/ed	p/ig
s/un	n/ap	b/ag

Ask students to tell what the word is. If they have difficulty, model the process for them: First say the word with the half-second delay (/s/ /at/), then repeat it several times with less and less time between the parts, until it is a recognizable word. It is also helpful to say the divided word in a phrase or sentence context; e.g., "The tomatoes were ripe and very /r/ /ed/." (See pages 113–114 for additional words.)

Eventually students will be ready to blend these words into three parts as well; i.e., initial consonant, vowel, and final consonant as in /n/ /a/ /p/. This is also called phonic blending (see page 75), and it is considerably more difficult than the blending illustrated above. It should be undertaken with patience and as much practice as necessary.

- Students should also be encouraged to segment words and have their classmates tell what the word is.

Phonemic Awareness: Manipulating Sounds in Words

- Explain that you are going to say a word and that they are to <u>drop the final sound</u> and say the new word back to you. For example, if you say *date*, they are to say *day*. Do the activity orally, without printing the words. Model the process with several words and then read others for them to respond to: *road (row), toad (toe), tied (tie), beet (bee), meal (me), tune (too), bike (by), lake (lay), soap (so), heat (he), sheet (she)*.

This activity is difficult for some children and should be approached with a game-like spirit, encouraging those who cannot do it to participate by echoing those who can. Students who are likely to be successful should be challenged to answer individually, and the whole class can then respond if they think the answer is correct.

- A similar activity asks students to drop the beginning sound of words; e.g., *cape (ape), fake (ache), shame (aim), dear (ear), bear (air), feet (eat), date (ate)*, etc.

Concept: Beginning Sounds in Words

- Practice auditory discrimination of initial sounds in words. Begin with sounds such as /m/, /s/, /r/, or /f/ because these are the easiest to elongate and separate from the rest of the word. First call attention to the sound (e.g., /s/), and ask students to listen for that sound as you say several words that begin with it: *sun, Sam, soft, super*. Then have students repeat the sound and give other words that begin with that sound.

- Read a list of words, many of which begin with the target sound while some do not. Have students respond to each word they hear that begins with the target sound. Their responses might be to say the sound aloud, clap, or stand up when they hear it.

- Ask students to think of words that begin with the target sound. Suggest one category such as "things in the classroom," "things in your kitchen," "things you play with," "places," "names of friends," etc., to help students focus their search for words.

- Make up a sentence with the children containing mostly words that begin with a given sound—similar to tongue twisters—and have students repeat them; e.g., "Five families fed forty foxes fine food."

- Initiate large class posters in the shape of some object beginning with the target sound; for instance, a sock for /s/, a rocket for /r/, a fan for /f/, or a moon for /m/. Encourage students to draw or cut out and paste pictures of objects whose names begin with the target sounds onto the appropriate poster. Or students may make their own book of sounds, one page per sound, following the same procedure.

Concept: Beginning Letters of Words

- Print a sentence six or seven words long on the chalkboard and read the sentence to the students; e.g., *Today we will meet the music teacher.* Point to the word *today* and tell the students that word begins with the letter [t]. Ask a student to circle other words that begin with the letter [t]. Continue for the other *beginning letters* [m] and [w]. You might have several students copy the beginning letters right under the words on the board. Establish that these are the *beginning letters* and encourage students to use the phrase as they show you beginning letters of words in books.

- While they are learning the alphabet, ask for the beginning letters of words you point to in their books or on the board such as the days of the week, the months, their names, titles of stories, etc.

Consonants: Letter-Sound Associations at the Beginnings of Words

- Ask students to give you words that begin with the target sound, for example, /f/. Print the words in a column on the board; then read them aloud. Ask what is the same about all the words you have printed. When it is established that they all begin with the same letter, [f], and the same sound, /f/, ask what sound the letter [f] stands for.

  Print a sentence on the chalkboard using several words that begin with the target sound; e.g., for /s/, *Save some seeds for Sam.* Read the sentence aloud pointing to each word. Point to and read one of the words beginning with the target sound (/s/) and ask students what sound they hear at the beginning of that word. Ask what letter is at the beginning of the word. Repeat with several words beginning with the same letter. Ask students to figure out what letter stands for that sound.

- Use a similar activity for several letter-sound associations and then print rhyming pairs of words on the chalkboard using the initial letters taught (e.g., if [s] and [m] have been taught, print *sail* and *mail*). Name one of the pair (e.g., *sail*) and ask an individual to point to the correct word.

- Have students write the letter for the beginning sounds of words you say aloud to them, or have them show you the correct letter card.

Consonants: Soft [c] and [g] Generalization

- On the board, print and say words beginning with "soft [c]" such as *circle, cent,* and *circus* and read them aloud. Ask for the beginning sound in each word and then ask what letter stands for /s/ at the beginning of these words ([c]). Remind the students that they have already learned that the letter [c] stands for /k/. Tell them that together you will figure out a rule to help them decide which sound to try for [c] at the beginning of a word. Write each word in the columns below, drawing a vertical line down the center as shown:

cent	circle	cyclone	candy	copy	cup
cell	city	cycle	card	contest	cuff

Ask students to figure out a rule for deciding when the letter [c] stands for /s/ and when [c] stands for /k/. If you need to prompt them, do so by asking what vowels follow the letter [c] in the soft [c] set (point to the words on the left). Have them look at the hard [c] set (point to the words on the right) and again ask for the vowels that follow the letter [c]. Draw circles around the first two letters in each of the words as students' answers are given.

Help students to come to the following generalization: **When [c] is followed by [e], [i], or [y], it usually stands for the soft sound (/s/); when [c] is followed by [a], [o] or [u], it stands for the hard sound (/k/).**

- Repeat the activity with the letter [g] using the following set of words:

gentle	giant	gym	gang	got	gum
germ	ginger	gypsy	gas	gong	gull

Note that the rule works for both letters.

When [c] or [g] is followed by [e], [i], or [y], it usually stands for the soft sound (/s/ or /j/); when [c] or [g] is followed by [a], [o], or [u], it stands for the hard sound (/k/ or /g/).

See word lists, page 122, for examples of this generalization, but note that several very common words that begin with [g] do not follow the rule: *get, gift, girl,* and *give*. It is important to encourage flexibility—students should try the sound according to the generalization and then try the other sound if the first attempt does not work.

Phonograms

- Show students how to write words based on the sounds in them. Print a consonant on the board (e.g., [m]), leave a little space, print a phonogram—a vowel plus consonant ending (e.g., [an] or [at]) and read it to the students; then model blending the two parts (/m/ /at/) with a half-second delay, and finally say the whole word (*mat*). Print a list of words under the word (*mat*) using the same phonogram (e.g., *b at, c at, f at, s at, p at, r at*). Point to each word and ask the students to give the sound for the initial consonant first, then for the phonogram, and then for the whole word.

- Playing *It's in the Bag:* Cut 3 × 5 index cards in half. Make two cards for each of the consonants [s], [m], [f], [b], [r], [t] and five cards for each of the phonograms; e.g., [at] and [it]. Put the consonants in one small paper bag and the phonograms in another. In turn, players first draw a letter from the consonant bag and keep it. On their next turn, they draw from the phonogram bag. If they can combine the two cards to make a real word, they keep the cards. If not, either the consonant or the phonogram is put back and the game continues with the next player. Players continue to draw and make words, or return their cards, until all the cards have been used. The player with the most words wins. Add more initial consonants and phonograms as they are learned.

Consonants: Consonant Substitution to Read and Write New Words

- Show students how to read and write new words using the consonant letter-sound associations they have learned plus the vowel-consonant endings of words, which are called *phonograms*. For instance, write the word *sat* on the board. Read it in two parts—/s/ /at/— then as the whole word, *sat*. Underline the [at] phonogram and ask who can read it. Then tell the students they can read other words that end in /at/ but begin with different consonants.

  Print the letter [m] on the board and give its sound, /m/. Leaving a little space, print [at] to the right of it and ask what the whole word is. Then erase the [m] in *mat* and substitute a [b]. Ask what the word is now. Have an individual come to the board, erase the first letter, substitute an [f], and read the new word. Proceed similarly, substituting [c], [h], [p], and [r]. Having students say the following couplet may help:

  Now erase the [s] in *sat*

  Put in an [f] and it says _____.

Repeat this strategy with other phonograms such as [ug], [an], [in], [ig], [en], [ot], [ub], etc.

- Print a word on the board and read it aloud. Then ask students to give a word that rhymes with it and begins with a specific sound. For example, print *cake* and ask a student for a word that rhymes with *cake* and begins with /m/. Print the word *make* when the student responds.

- Print a one-syllable word containing a phonogram on the board and underline the phonogram. Ask students to print other words with the same ending on their papers. For instance, print *bug* and ask students to write *tug, rug, mug, dug, hug*. Be sure to ask only for words beginning with consonants that have already been taught.

Hearing Medial Vowels

- Introduce a targeted short vowel in medial position by reading about eight or nine words, some of which contain that vowel sound. Ask students to respond when they hear the target sound. For instance, they can listen for /ă/ in the words *map, make, tack, Sam, send, sit, fast, fade, mask,* and respond by clapping when they hear it.

- Say aloud a short vowel (CVC) word, then segment it, exaggerating the medial vowel; for instance, *man* said as /m/ /a/ /n/. Ask what sound they hear in the middle of the word. Have students say the word aloud with you, exaggerating the vowel sound. Repeat the process with another word containing a different short vowel; for instance, *men*.

- Read a list of short vowel (CVC) words that contain only two different short vowels; for instance, *pan, pat, pen, mess, tank, ten, ranch, sand, send.* Ask students to give the vowel sound for each word you read. After several vowel letter-sound associations have been taught, increase the number of vowels included in the words in this listening activity.

- In a paper bag or envelope, put small pictures of objects with one-syllable names that have short vowels. For instance, for /ă/ you might have pictures of a man, pan, map, cat, flag, hat, hand, etc., and for /ĭ/, you might choose pictures of a pig, mitt, pin, lips, etc.

  Spend just a few minutes each day naming the objects and confirming what the medial vowel is. Encourage students to find more pictures, have the class agree which vowel they hear in the middle, and add them to the collection. Also add more pictures as new vowels are taught.

Medial Vowels: Letter-Sound Associations

- Teach one vowel at a time. It could be introduced in a phonogram. For instance, ask the students what sound they hear in the middle of a set of [at] words (*sat, bat, rat,* etc.) that are written on the chalkboard. Then ask what letter stands for /ă/ in these words.

- Give students lined paper, numbered 1–10. Ask them to listen as you read a list of words. They are to write the letter [a] beside the numbers for words when they hear the /ă/ sound. Read a list of ten short CVC words, some of which contain the sound /ă/:

  1. *map*
  2. *net*
  3. *man*
  4. *dip*
  5. *bag*
  6. *tap*
  7. *pack*
  8. *sick*
  9. *fan*
  10. *gas*

- After teaching several vowels, dictate simple CVC words using only the vowels and consonants you have worked with. Students are to write the words. (See word lists, page 113.)

- Print phrase cards (or list phrases on the chalkboard) for students to copy and illustrate: *a cat in a cap, a fat dog, a big man, a wet mop, a sad pig, a hot dog,* etc. Students may be encouraged also to write a story about their pictures.

Phonic Blending

- Begin practice in phonic blending by printing a CVC word on the board, e.g., *fan.* Ask what the word is and then say, "Yes. The word is *fan.* But if you did not know it, you could give the sound for each letter and then put the sounds together to read the word." Model the blending by pointing to individual letters and giving the sounds they stand for separated by less than a half second: /m/ /a/ /n/. Ask students to give the sounds with you as you do it several times—faster each time until you are all saying the word *man.*

Write *map, fit, sat, sip, fan,* and *rip* on the board and say, "You can put the sounds together and tell me what the words are. Let's do them together: /m/ /a/ /p/, *map*; /f/ /i/ /t/, *fit*; /s/ /i/ /t/, *sit*; etc." Point to words randomly and ask volunteers to give the sounds and the words.

See word lists for other CVC words to practice blending, or use nonsense words. End each blending practice by having students respond quickly, reading the words practiced (without blending). Incorporate the words into phrases for students to read: *big map, sad rat, pet the red hen, Dad had a wet hat,* etc.

Consonant Blends

• Print the letter combinations [bl], [cl], [fl], and [pl] in a column on the board. Tell the students that these are called *consonant blends* because we blend the sounds of the consonants together. Ask them to listen as you say the first one, /bl/, and then ask them to listen for the consonant blend in the word *black* as you write it on the board beside the [bl]. Say other words that begin with /bl/: *blue, blond, blaze*. Ask someone to say the next consonant blend as you point to [cl]; confirm /kl/ and write the word *clam* beside it as you read the word with them. Proceed similarly for [fl] to /fl/ in *flag*, and [pl] to /pl/ in *plum*. Then ask students to read the following words printed on the board and use them in sentences: *blob, plan, clip, blip, flip, plus, clap, flap.*

• Ask for rhyming words in the following way: Print [fl] on the board and point to it. Say, "I want you to give me a word that begins with these letters [do not give the consonant blend orally] and rhymes with the word *tea*. [Do not write the word; give it orally. Wait for students' response.] Yes, *flea* rhymes with *tea* and begins with the letters [fl]." Suggestions for other consonant blends and rhyming words follow:

[fl] "tea" [flea]	[cl] "dock" [clock]	[fl] "tame" [flame]
[pl] "bait" [plate]	[bl] "go" [blow]	[cl] "time" [climb]

Select initial consonant blends from lists on pages 115–117.

Consonant Digraphs

By the time consonant digraphs are taught, the students have probably seen and read many of them in their books. The concept that two-letter consonant combinations can stand for one sound, a sound that is different from either one of the two letters alone, is made more explicit as students focus on the association between the sounds /ch/, /sh/, and /th/ and the letters that represent them.

- Ask the students to tell you the beginning sound they hear as you say these words: *children, chalk, checker, chicken.* Confirm their answer, /ch/. Then print on the board: *check, chin, chap.* Read the words to the class. Ask what sound is heard at the beginning of each and ask what letters represent that /ch/ sound ([c] and [h]). Explain that [ch] stands for a different sound than either [c] or [h]. Ask students to clap their hands if they hear /ch/ at the beginning of each word you say: *chicken, show, champion, clapping, shell, chowder, choose, thunder, cheese.*

- Use the same procedure to introduce the [sh] to /sh/ association. Then you may ask students to guess the word that begins with either /ch/ or /sh/ to answer definitions you provide. Give clues something like the following:

If you are not tall, you may be . . . [*short*].

If you are not a grown-up, you are probably a . . . [*child*].

If you need to dig a hole, you might want to use a . . . [*shovel*].

A very large fish with sharp teeth might be a . . . [*shark*].

You may want to keep all your tools in a tool . . . [*chest*] or [*shed*].

See additional words, page 120.

Long Vowel Words with Final [e]

- Review the five short vowel sounds the students have already learned and remind them that these are called short vowels. Explain that vowel letters stand for more than one sound and that they will now be learning the long vowel sounds. Each long vowel sound is the same as the name of the letter. "The long vowel sound of [a] is . . ." (wait for students to respond with /ā/), "the long vowel sound for [e] is . . ." and so on.

- Pronounce the following words slowly and tell students to listen for the long [ā] in each one: *made, lame, late, bake, lace.* Have students repeat each word after you, elongating the vowel.

- Tell some riddles. The answers should have the long vowel [a]. When someone guesses correctly, write the word on the board.

It is a girl's name that rhymes with *face.* [*Grace*]

It is a body of water, larger than a pond and smaller than most oceans. [*lake*]

It describes a person who has to use a cane or crutches. He or she is . . . [*lame*].

- Read the following word pairs to the students after writing them on the board. For each pair, ask what is different about the way the two words are written and the way they are pronounced: mad, made; hat, hate; rat, rate; tam, tame. (There is an [e] on the end of one word in the pair and not on the other. Also, one word has the short vowel sound and one has the long vowel sound.) Then have students figure out why the vowel is short in the first word and long in the second. (The second word has an [e] on the end of it.) Tell them we call it the magic [e]. Coach them in figuring out this generalization (described earlier as the "magic [e] rule"): **When a short word ends with an [e], the first vowel has the long sound and the final [e] is silent.**

- For another activity, you might print short CVC words and CVCe words on cards for the students to read to each other and separate into two piles—one for short vowel words and one for long vowel words. (See page 125 for a list of contrasting CVC and CVCe words.)

- Or, print directions on the board for students to follow. Include long and short vowel words (CVC and CVCe) in the directions. For instance:

Make a cane with black stripes on it.

Make a man on a bike.

Make a snake with a big hat.

Hearing Syllables in Words

- Introduce *syllables* by having students hear and see the two parts of compound words. Ask for the two parts in the words *cowboy, streetlight, treetop,* and have the children say the two parts aloud. You might give further practice by having them clap once or twice according to the number of parts they hear in the following words: *pan, pancake, tea, teapot, may, maybe, today, homework.*

Praise the students' efforts and then tell them you will challenge them with some words that also have two parts, but the two parts are not little words, they are *syllables*. Ask them to clap once for one syllable and twice for two syllables as you read the following list: *day, paper, candy, grass, finger, table, polite, cool, tackle.*

Complete the lesson of listening to syllables in words by having students clap once, twice, or three times, depending on how many parts they hear in each word. Read the following list, being sure to enunciate each syllable clearly, but do not pause between syllables: go, di/vide, mul/ti/ply, skel/e/ton, send, sen/tence, fast, pol/i/tics, po/lice.

Syllabication: CVC/CVC Words

- Explain to students that the way to read a long word is to break it into syllables, say each syllable separately, and then say them together.

  Print *blanket* on the board. Ask how many syllables students hear when you read the word *blanket* (two). What are they? (/blan/ /ket/). Print the two syllables separately under the word and point out that each has a vowel in it. Ask, "What vowel sound do we hear in each syllable?" (/ă/ in the first and /ĕ/ in the second). We hear a short vowel sound in each part. Proceed similarly with the word hunter. Then give the generalization: **When a word has two consonants between two vowels** (point to each), **divide the word between the two consonants** (draw a line between the [n] and [k] in *blanket*) **and try the short sound for the first vowel.**

  Then print *tennis* on the board and ask someone to read it aloud. Point to the two consonants and two vowels as you mention them in giving the generalization again. Ask individual students to divide the following words and read them aloud: *kitten, pencil, basket, sunset.*

- For another lesson, you might print the word *triplets* on the board and ask a student to "teach" it to the class.

  See word lists, pages 140-142 for other words to have students syllabicate and read.

[y] as a Vowel

- Tell the students that the letter [y] is usually a vowel at the end of words. Ask them to listen to the words you say and tell what vowel sound they hear at the end of each. Print each word on the board as the vowel sound is identified. Print them in two columns—those that end with the long [i] in one column and those with long [e] in the second. Use these words: *fly, shy, funny, nutty, try, dusty, spy, bumpy, sly, happy, crusty, my, by, bunny, dry, grumpy.* When all the words have been printed, ask what sound the [y] stands for in the words in the first column and print "long i" over that column. Similarly, elicit "long e" and print it over the second column.

Ask a volunteer to go to the board and find those words that have more than one syllable and then divide those words into syllables. After the divisions, ask if anyone can give a rule that tells when the letter [y] at the end of a word stands for long [i] and when it stands for long [e]. If necessary, give a hint that it has to do with words that have one syllable or two. Elicit the generalization: **When the letter [y] comes at the end of a one-syllable word, it often stands for the long [i] sound. When it comes at the end of a word with more than one syllable, it usually stands for the long [e] sound.**

- Give each pair of students one word printed on paper. Tell them to write a riddle for their word. The first sentence in each riddle should give a definition of the word. The second should give the first syllable of the word. The third sentence should ask: "What am I?" For example, for the word *fifty*, the riddle might be: "I am half of one hundred. My first syllable is /fif/. What am I?" After the children working in pairs have completed their riddles, have a riddle time. The authors read their riddles and the class guesses the answers. Use the following words to reinforce two-syllable words and words ending in [y]: *rusty, funny, tunnel, candy, magnet, penny, puppy, jelly, attic, twenty, button.*

See lists, page 126 for words to use in other activities.

Vowels Followed by [r]

Learning that **a vowel followed by [r] stands for a special sound** will give students the knowledge to decode a great many more words.

- Print the following columns of words on the board:

cat	car
fat	far
stack	star

Have different children read the words in the first column as you point to them. Ask the children what vowel sound they hear in the words in the first column (short [a]). Next, read aloud to the students the words in the second column as you point to them. Ask if the vowel sound is the same as in the words in the first column. Now have students read the words in the second column aloud with you. Point out that the words in this column all have the letter [a] followed by [r]. Explain that the vowel letter

[a] followed by [r] has its own special sound, /ar/ as in *car* and *star*. Then ask if anyone can think of any words that rhyme with *car, far,* and *star.* Print them on the board as they are mentioned. (Possibilities include *tar, bar, par, jar, mar, scar, char, cigar, ajar.*)

- Use the same procedure for [or], and [er], [ir], and [ur]. After these have been taught, you might ask students to write sentences and illustrate them using the following words which you print on the board: *nurse, fern, bird, farm, card, clerk, fur, stork, shirt, short.*

Word lists will be found on page 127.

Silent Consonants

- Print these sentences on the chalkboard:

He did not take a bath.

This string has a knot in it.

Have a volunteer read the first sentence. Then ask students to listen to each word as you read the second sentence: Read it and underline the word *knot.* Ask students to read the word *knot* again. Have a volunteer come to the board and underline the word *not* in the first sentence. Ask: "Do the two words sound the same? Do they look the same? What is different about them?" (*knot* in the second sentence has the letter [k] in front of the letter [n]).

Use the same procedure with the words *ring* and *wring* in two sentences:

She will ring the bell at five o'clock.

She will wring out the wet socks.

Compare the words and have students notice that the word *wring,* meaning to squeeze water out, is spelled with a [w] in front of the [r].

After reading the two lists of words given below, have students give a rule about words that begin with [kn]. **When a word begins with [kn], the [k] is silent but we give the sound /n/.** Similarly elicit the rule for words that begin with [wr]: **When a word begins with [wr], the [w] is silent but we give the sound /r/.**

knot	wrong
knife	write
knit	wren

Noun Inflections: Plurals

- Give students practice in making plurals. Explain that *plurals* are words that mean "more than one." Give concrete examples. Show a book and say, "This is one _____" (*book*). Then show three and say, "Now I have three _____" (*books*). Give a similar example with drinking glasses. Focus the students' attention on the two ways to make plurals: by adding /s/, as in *books* and by adding /es/ as in *glasses*. Point out that if we say them differently, we must print them differently also. We add [s] to some words, and we add [es] to other words. Ask who can tell how we know which to add—an [s] or an [es]. Confirm that all we have to do is to say the plural word and listen to it closely.

- Write the following words on the board and ask students to say the plurals aloud and then write them on their papers: *map, box, cup, clip, fox, brush, sled, dish.*

Verb Inflections: [ed], [ing], [s]

- Print the following words in a column on the board: *mix, mixing, mixed.* Read the words to the class, emphasizing and underlining the [ing] and [ed] endings. Explain that many action words have an ending added to them so they will give the correct meaning. For instance you might ask, "If you are fishing, you would not say, 'I am fish today,' would you? What would you say? [I am fish<u>ing</u> today.] And if you went fishing yesterday in the pond, you would say . . . [Yesterday I fish<u>ed</u> in the pond]." Print the following sentences on the board:

  Fred is filling the hole with stones.
  Fred filled the hole.

  Ask students to read the two sentences and have a student point to the one that tells something that is happening now. Have it read aloud. Point out the [ing] on the word *filling* and say that [ing] tells us the action is happening now. Have the second sentence read aloud. Ask if it says Fred is still trying to fill the hole. Establish that, no, he worked on it in the past and that an [ed] ending tells us that the action has already happened.

- Print the following words in a column on the board: *smile, smiling, smiled.* Ask a student to circle the [ing] and the [ed]. Ask students to figure out what happened to the word *smile* when the endings were added. (The final [e] was dropped.) Explain that this is what happens to long vowel (CVCe) words when [ing] or [ed] is added. Ask if the vowel sound changes when the [e] is dropped and these endings are added. Explain that the vowel stays long, just as it was. Demonstrate by printing base words on the chalkboard. Ask individuals to come to the board, read one of them, and then write the same word with [ing] and [ed] added. Use the following words: *hope, skate, shave.* Ask other students to say a sentence using the words that have been written to reinforce the understanding that [ing] signifies something that is happening now and [ed] signifies something that has happened in the past.

Also see word lists, pages 130–131.

Vowel Digraphs

- Read the following riddles and inform students that the correct answers are long [a] words. As correct answers are given, write the words on the board in two columns, one for [ay] and one for [ai].

  This is the opposite of night (*day*).
  This is the part of a boat that the wind pushes to make it go (*sail*).
  This runs on a track and you can take a ride on it (*train*).
  This is the opposite of work (*play*).

  Read the two words in the first column, stressing the long vowel sound. Ask what letters must stand for the long [a] sound in these words. Confirm that [ay] stands for /ā/. Then read the words in the second column and confirm that the letters [ai] also stand for the long [a] sound. Compare the two lists and elicit from the students that [ay] is used for /ā/ at the end of words and that [ai] is used in the middle of words.

- Print the following words on the board and have individual students read them: *pay, lay, ray, stay, clay, wait, train, jail, snail, maid.*

- Write the following phrases on the board. Have students copy them and draw appropriate pictures: *six snails, a gray kitten, a dog at play,* and *a sharp nail.*

  See word lists, page 132, for developing further activities.

Variant Vowel Digraphs and Diphthongs

- Ask students to listen to the words you say and tell what vowel sound they hear. Say *peak, leap, beach* (long [e]). Print the words in a column on the board. Then ask them to listen to the following words and tell you again what vowel sound they hear: *head, breath, spread* (short [e]). Print the words in a second column on the board. Ask a student to circle the letters that stand for the long [e] in the first column and the letters that stand for the short [e] in the second column. Establish that [ea] can stand for the long [e] sound and also for the short [e] sound. Suggest that when they see a word they do not recognize that has the letters [ea], they should try the long [e] sound first because more [ea] words have that sound. If the long [e] sound does not make a sensible word, they should try the short [e] sound.

- Print these words on the board and ask individuals to read them: *peach, squeal, bread, treat, deaf, sweater.* Offer help as the students discuss whether using the long [e] sound makes a real word. Encourage flexibility and ask students for a sentence after they agree on the word.

- In a playful spirit you might do the same for the word *read* which can be read both ways.

- Print word frames on the board and have volunteers take turns at the board printing [ea] in one of them, reading the word, and using it in a sentence. Suggested frames: *t__ch, w__lth, s__m, thr__d, cl__n.*

- Write sentences on the board using words with [ow]. Students are to fold a paper in half lengthwise and write *crow* at the top of one column and *crowd* at the top of the other. Confirm that this has been done correctly. Ask students to read the sentences, find the [ow] words, and copy them on their papers putting the words in which [ow] sounds as it does in *crow* in that column. Words in which [ow] sounds as it does in *crowd* should be written in the column under *crowd*. See word lists, pages 135-139 for words to use in the sentences. Here are a few suggestions:

My red and yellow hat has blown away.

The brown and white cow gives the best milk.

The black crow will fly down from the tree.

How will you know what to do?

The circus clowns are coming to town.

- Print the following words on the board and call on a volunteer to be teacher and show how to decode them: *pillow, flower, arrow, feather.* Encourage syllable division between the two middle consonants as a first step. After the words have been taught, ask for volunteers to put them into sentences.

Syllabication: CV/CVC and CVC/VC Words

- Write the following words on the board, divide them into syllables, and ask the students to read them aloud with you:

pa/per   hu/man   o/pen

From these known words and with your encouragement, students can infer the rule governing the long vowel in the first syllable. Ask how many consonants there are in the middle of these words (one). Ask where you divided the words—before or after the consonant (before). Ask if the first syllable of each word is long or short (long). Then ask why. (There is no consonant after the vowel in the first syllable, so the vowel is long.)

Prompt students to give the generalization: **If a word has only one consonant in the middle, divide the word <u>before</u> that consonant and try the long sound for the vowel.** Explain that the rule does not always work, but it will give them a real word more than half of the time, as in *bacon, clover, diner, diver, frozen,* etc. **If the long sound does not work, they should divide the word <u>after</u> the middle consonant and try the short vowel sound for the first vowel** as in *habit, lemon, lizard,* etc. (See lists beginning on page 140.)

- Students might do a word search in old newspapers or magazines for examples of two-syllable words with only one consonant in the middle. They can start two lists on the bulletin board—one for the long vowel words (*ro/bot*) and one for the short vowel words (*rob/in*).

Syllabication: Words Ending in C[le]

- Write the following sentence on the board, underlining the words *apple* and *maple*:

Can you pick an <u>apple</u> from a <u>maple</u> tree?

Divide *ap/ple* and *ma/ple*, making the [ple] the second syllable. Have a student read the sentence and explain why the [a] is short in the word *apple* and long in the word *maple*. (Because in *apple,* the first syllable ends with a consonant, but in *maple,* the first syllable ends in a vowel.)

Tell students that a consonant plus [le] at the end of a word (C[le]) is usually a syllable. That is, we divide the word before that consonant (as in *tat/tle, ta/ble*). If the first syllable ends in a consonant, we try the short sound for the first vowel (e.g., *tat/tle*). If the first syllable ends in a vowel, we try the long sound (e.g., *ma/ple*).

Ask individuals to divide the following words into syllables, read them aloud, and use them in sentences: *dimple, cycle, humble, stable, pebble, ladle, noble, gentle.*

- Ask students to write rhymes using one of the following pairs of words written on the board: *able, table; rumble, tumble; rattle, tattle; cable, fable.*

See word lists, page 142, for developing other activities.

Two-Syllable Words with Digraphs

- Review vowel digraphs in single-syllable words, if necessary, before introducing the two-syllable words. Then write *dainty, coaster, payment, mermaid,* and *display* on the board. Remind students that both vowels in vowel digraphs remain in the same syllable. Ask individuals to put a slash mark between the two syllables of each word, read it, and use it in a sentence. Ask each student how he or she decided where to divide the word and how he or she knew what the word was.

- Ask students to try to write the nonsense words you dictate which will all have either the long [a] or the long [o] sound. There are different ways to spell each word. Create an atmosphere of interest and fun. For example, show how you might write the word *tail: tail* or *tale* but probably not *tayl* because we usually find *ay* at the end of words or syllables, not in the middle of them. Give examples of real words in which the long [a] sound is spelled differently (for example, [ai] as in *maid,* [aCe] as in *sale*). Do the same for the long [o] sound ([oCe] as in *role,* [oa] as in *goal,* or just [o] if there is no consonant following it, as in *go*).

Ask students to write each nonsense word you dictate two different ways. Do the first one with them as an example. Then dictate the following words:

/zap·bān/ (may be spelled *zapbain, zapbane*)

/hob·tōk/ (may be spelled *hobtoak, hobtoke*)

/fin·dāl/ (may be spelled *findail, findale*)

/jō·brip/ (may be spelled *jobrip, joebrip, joabrip*)

/tō·spā/ (may be spelled *toaspay, toespay, towspay*)

/mat·rōd/ (may be spelled *matroad, matrode*)

Have the spellings written on the board by individuals, who should explain why they spelled each word as they did. Remind students that this is all just for the fun of it. No answers are really "correct" or "wrong," but some are more possible than others.

Prefixes and Suffixes

- Students should be made aware that word parts called *prefixes* and *suffixes* can be added to words they already know. If students know the meanings of the *prefixes* and *suffixes,* they will be able to read and understand, and also write, many additional words.

  Print these sentences on the board:

  Did you tie that package?

  Yes, but it came untied on the bus.

  We better retie it before its contents fall out.

  Read the sentences aloud with students and ask if anyone can figure out what *un* means in *untied*. Confirm that it means "not" or "the opposite of" *tied*. Ask for the meaning of *re* in *retie*. Confirm that it means "to do something again."

  Explain that *re* and *un* are prefixes. When they are added to base words, we get a new word with a different meaning—*rename* means "to name again," *unclean* means "not clean," etc.

- Print a sentence on the board, leaving a space to the left of a base word where a student is to fill in the prefix *un* or *re* to fit the definition you give. For example, write *They __loaded the truck,* and ask for the word that means the truck was not loaded (*unloaded*). Or ask for the word that means they had to load the truck again (*reloaded*). Another example: Write *The cat was __wise to chase that chipmunk up the tree,* Ask for the word that means the cat was not wise (*unwise*).

- Similar activities should be undertaken for suffixes. For example, print base words on the chalkboard and have the students read them aloud: *rest, quick, thank, forget*. Then print the suffixes *less, ly, ful,* and *ness* on the board. Point to the base word *rest* and ask students to add a suffix to it to make a word that means "full of rest." Students should then print the suffixed word on their papers (*restful*). Do the same with the remaining base words using appropriate definitions to include all the suffixes.

- After students are comfortable with several prefixes and suffixes, present further activities that include both prefixes and suffixes.

- Ask students to assemble word parts that fit sentences you read. Print *help, pain, harm, less,* and *ful* on five large word cards. Give the cards to five children, who should stand in front of the group in random order. Read aloud a sentence with a missing word (for examples, see below) and ask a volunteer to give a word that makes sense made from any two of the five word parts in the sentence. Then the two students with the word parts stand together, and the group decides if the correct word has been formed. The two then stand back and you read the next sentence. There are many sentence possibilities, which might include the following:

My brother can't swim. He is _____ in the water.

A broken arm can be very _____.

Words from the lists on pages 143–145 may be used to develop additional activities.

Word Patterns

• Students already know many of the words reviewed as examples of word patterns. It is helpful, nevertheless, to call attention to the patterns as it will help the students transfer that knowledge to new and longer words.

Write the following phrases on the board and ask students to read them aloud with you: *wild west, kind mother, left and right.* Underline *wild, kind,* and *right.* Ask what the vowel sound is in these words (long [i]). Explain that in words with *ild, ind,* and *igh*, the [i] is usually long. Have volunteers circle these patterns in the words on the board and then think together of other words with the same pattern. Write them on the board. (See word lists, page 147.)

Follow the same procedure with the long [o] pattern words: *c<u>old</u> snow, horse and c<u>olt</u>, <u>post</u> office.* (See word lists, page 148.)

Remind students that they need to pay attention to the meaning of what they are reading to know when these letter combinations signal a long [i] or [o] and when they do not. Write the following sentences, underscoring as shown, and have them read aloud:

The north <u>wind</u> was <u>cold</u>.

Be careful not to <u>wind</u> the <u>old</u> clock too <u>tightly</u>.

• Students might choose three rhyming words using any of these patterns and write their own silly rhymes or silly sentences. These should be pure nonsense to be enjoyed, not analyzed. A starter might be: *The most scary ghost played host at the post office,* or *She was so cold, She had to scold, The man so bold, Who went and sold, Her warm coat of gold.*

3. SUGGESTIONS FOR ASSESSING STUDENT PROGRESS AND PROVIDING FOR REMEDIAL INSTRUCTION

General Guidelines

Teacher assessment of student progress has always been considered important in enhancing student achievement. It is thought even more important now than in previous years. (See California's Curriculum Plan, 1995.)

The following suggestions are designed to help the teacher determine whether students have learned the phonic concepts, phonic elements, and generalizations they have been taught. The forms of assessment vary, and they may be adapted and modified to suit the needs of the teacher and the students. Generally, forms where students read the target words aloud are more valid than forms where they circle a word read by you.* Other forms of assessment may be used, as well as your own estimate of how well the student is learning.

For most of the assessments proposed we have suggested the number of correct (or incorrect) items that indicates adequate (or inadequate) performance.

Each test should be given after students have been introduced to and have practiced the particular elements or generalizations. It is important to have an early estimate of whether students have learned what has been taught or are in need of further instruction.

In general, it is best to treat the tests as if they were regular exercises. You might introduce each by telling students that today they will do an exercise that will help find out what they have learned and what still needs to be learned.

For the younger children (kindergarten and grade 1), groups of no more than ten or so should be tested at one time. This will make it easier to observe individuals and to see how well they are following directions. For older students (grades 2 to 4), larger groups may be tested together as long as students can attend to the task and follow directions.

Provide each student with a pencil and paper. Establish quiet and attention.

---

*Throughout, the term *target word* is used to indicate the word to be read, written, or selected from alternatives by the student. It is usually underlined.

Ask students to print their names at the top of their papers and to wait quietly until all have finished doing so. Then start the exercise.

Print Concepts

(This is appropriate for kindergarten and for less mature students in grade 1.)

Identifying Sentences, Words, and Letters

Students are to identify a printed sentence, a word, letters, and beginning letters in words. This can be done informally with individual children. Ask the child to underline or circle with his or her finger a sentence, a word, and a letter in a familiar book.

Print several short sentences on the board and ask the student to frame or circle a sentence and then count the words in it. Point to a word and ask the student to count the letters in it. Finally, ask him or her to point to the beginning letters of several words.

Concepts of Alphabet, Capital Letters, and Lowercase Letters

These also may be assessed informally as you point to any display of the alphabet in the classroom or a book and ask the students what the whole group of letters together is called. Similarly, point to individual letters and ask if they are capital letters or lowercase letters.

Alphabetic Writing

Printing Capital Letters from Dictation*

Pass out papers and ask children to print their name on top, then to print the numbers 1 to 7 down the left side. Demonstrate on the board how the page is to look, or give them pages already numbered.

---

*If a student can print letters from dictation, he or she can probably recognize and name letters. When a student is unable to print letters from dictation, check on his or her ability to recognize letters (point to letters as you name them) and to name letters (name them as you point to them). Poor performance on matching upper- and lowercase letters (see page 91, this section) is another indication that the student has not learned his or her letters well enough.

Say: Next to number 1, print capital E. Next to number 2, print capital K.

1. E
2. K
3. D
4. G

5. B
6. I
7. H

Continue in this manner for all the letters, preceding each with the label "capital." Test only the letters that have been taught—a set of 7 to 10 letters at a time, until all letters are done.

Scoring:

Adequate = 6 to 7 correct out of 7 (8, 9, or 10 correct out of 10).
Inadequate = 5 or fewer correct out of 7 (7 or fewer correct out of 10).

Printing Lowercase Letters from Dictation

Pass out papers and ask children to print their name on top, then the numbers 1 to 7 down the left side. Demonstrate on the board how the page is to look, or give them pages already numbered.

Say: You are now going to print seven lowercase letters. Listen carefully and print the lowercase letter next to each number I say. Next to number 1, print lowercase o, (etc.).

1. o
2. l
3. n
4. h

5. j
6. m
7. p

Continue in this manner, testing 7 to 10 letters at a time, until all the letters learned are tested.

Scoring:

Adequate = 6 to 7 correct out of 7 (8, 9, or 10 correct out of 10).
Inadequate = 5 or fewer correct out of 7 (7 or fewer correct out of 10).

Matching Capital and Lowercase Letters

On 8½" x 11" sheets of paper print seven capital letters down the left side and seven lowercase equivalents down the right, in mixed order. Duplicate and distribute. Ask students to match each capital letter to its lowercase letter. Do the first letter with them.

A	e
B	a
C	f
D	b
E	d
F	c
G	g

Test only those practiced in class and test only seven letters at a time. The same format can be used for the remaining sets of letters.

Scoring:

Adequate = 6 to 7 correct out of 7.
Inadequate = 5 or fewer correct out of 7.

Phonemic Awareness

Rhyming Words

Distribute 8½″ × 11″ sheets of paper. After students have written their names, ask them to print the numbers 1 to 10 down the left side.

Say: We are going to do some rhyming words. Listen to the two words I say. If the two words rhyme, if they sound the same at the end—print a "Y" for yes. If the two words do not rhyme, print an "N" for no.

Do the first two as examples together with the entire group. Emphasize word endings clearly and repeat each pair as instructed below.

Say: The two words are *pen* and *ten*. Does *pen* rhyme with *ten*? Yes, so on your paper print a "Y" for yes next to number 1.

Let's do another together. The two words are *fox* and *dog*. Do *fox* and *dog* rhyme? No, so you would print an "N" for no next to number 2. (Be sure all have done the samples correctly.)

Now listen carefully to the words and do these by yourself. Number 3: *shoe . . . foot*. Print a "Y" for yes if the words rhyme and an "N" for no if they do not rhyme; *shoe . . . foot*.

Read the remaining word pairs in the same manner. The words are not to be seen by the students.

1.	pen	ten (sample)
2.	fox	dog (sample)
3.	shoe	foot
4.	hat	cat
5.	hand	thumb

6. cane	rain
7. goat	boat
8. pup	bug
9. play	may
10. mop	top

Scoring:

Adequate = 8 or more correct out of 10 (counting sample items).

Inadequate = 7 or fewer correct out of 10 (counting sample items).

Letter-to-Sound Associations

Associating Consonant Letters with Sounds at the Beginning of Words

Have students print the numbers 1 to 10 down the left side of their papers.

Say: Beside each number print the letter for the beginning sound you hear in each word I say. Let's do number 1 together. What is the sound you hear at the beginning of the word *mouse* (pause) *mouse?* What letter would you print? Yes, print [m] beside the number 1. That's good.

Let's do number 2 together. What is the first sound you hear in the word *bike* (pause) *bike?* What letter stands for that sound? [b], that is fine. Print [b] beside number 2. (Be sure all have done the samples correctly.) Now you do these by yourself.

Proceed with the following words, saying each twice.

1. mouse (sample)			2. bike (sample)		
3. fun	4. tell		5. song	6. run	
7. tie	8. ball		9. road	10. face	

Test the remaining sets of consonants as they are taught using your own choice of words.

Scoring:

Adequate = 8 or more correct (counting sample items).

Inadequate = 7 or fewer correct (counting sample items).

Consonant Substitution

Students should number down their papers 1 to 6. Print *sad* on the chalkboard.

Say: This word is *sad.* The word begins with the letter [s] that stands for the sound /s/. It ends with /ă/-/d/, /ăd/ and so the word is

/s/-/ad/ /sad/. Print the word *sad* next to number 1 on your paper. Now, next to number 2, print the word *mad*; next to number 3, print the word *bad*. And next to number 4, print the word *fad*. Number 5, print *had*; and next to 6 print *dad*.

Other consonant substitutions can be assessed using different endings. See the short vowel (CVC) word lists, pages 113–115 in the Appendix, but be sure to use only words with beginning consonants that have been taught. (Other word lists referred to in this chapter can all be found in the Appendix.) Try to include at least four different consonants with the same ending as the first word you print for them. For example, print *tan* and sound it out as above. Ask students to copy *tan* and then ask them to print *fan, man, pan, ran*.

Scoring:

Adequate = 5 out of 6 correct, or 4 out of 5 correct (including the sample).

Inadequate = 4 or fewer correct out of 6, or 3 or fewer out of 5.

Identifying CVC Words

This can be assessed several ways:

1. On an 8½" × 11" sheet of paper print the numbers 1 to 10 down the left side. Beside each number print any ten of the following twenty sets of three words—a target word and two alternatives (as shown below). Omit underlining target words on student copies and use only sets with the consonants and short words that have been taught. Or you may create your own sets: three words in each set, at least one with the same initial consonant as the target word.

Duplicate the list for each student. Ask them to circle, on each line, the target word that you read. Read words that will sample the short vowels.

1.	<u>cab</u>	can	tab
2.	bid	<u>bad</u>	bat
3.	<u>tag</u>	tan	bag
4.	tap	ham	<u>tam</u>
5.	rim	fan	<u>ran</u>
6.	lap	<u>nap</u>	nip
7.	<u>bib</u>	big	bat
8.	dip	<u>dim</u>	dad
9.	<u>sip</u>	sap	sit
10.	nip	man	<u>map</u>
11.	win	bed	<u>web</u>

12.	van	<u>vet</u>	wet
13.	him	ham	<u>hen</u>
14.	<u>job</u>	jig	jam
15.	<u>nip</u>	hip	nap
16.	hot	dig	<u>dot</u>
17.	got	<u>gum</u>	sum
18.	sob	<u>sub</u>	sad
19.	<u>bus</u>	gas	bit
20.	hip	top	<u>hop</u>

Scoring:

Adequate = 7 or more correct out of 10.

Inadequate = 6 or fewer correct out of 10.

2. Another form, somewhat harder, is to ask students to print CVC words that you dictate. Use only the consonants and short vowels that have been taught.

3. Or you might duplicate a list of short vowel (CVC) words containing only the consonants and vowels taught thus far. Students may read the list aloud individually to you. A longer list may be read by a group of students, one word per student, as you take notes on who makes what errors. Flash cards can be made and used in the same manner.

Beginning Consonant Blends

Distribute paper to the students. Ask them to print their names and then the numbers 1 to 10 down the left side.

Say: I am going to say some words, and I want you to listen carefully for the first two sounds you hear. Then print the two letters for the first two sounds.

Let's do two together. The word is *brown*. What two sounds do you hear at the beginning of *brown*? Yes, /br/. Now what two letters stand for the sounds /br/? Yes, [br]. Print [br] beside number 1 on your paper.

Let's do another together. The word is *clock*. Think of the first two sounds in *clock*. What two letters stand for these sounds? [cl], yes, so print [cl] beside number 2 on your paper.

Now do the same for each of these words: number 3, print the beginning sounds for *cream* (etc.).

1. brown (sample)
2. clock (sample)
3. cream
4. plane
5. snap
6. grape

7. speed	9. fly	
8. brand	10. glad	

Scoring:

Adequate = 7 out of 10 correct, including the samples.
Inadequate = 6 or fewer correct, including the samples.

Consonant Digraphs

This can be assessed in several ways:

1. On 8½″ × 11″ paper, print any ten of the following twenty-three sets of three words—a target word and two alternatives (as shown below). (Omit underlining target words on student copies.) Students are to circle the words you read. In selecting your word sets, choose those with target words to include initial [ch], [sh], [th], [wh], and final [th], [ch], and [sh].

1. cage	shame	change
2. choke	shake	cake
3. cop	chop	shop
4. shall	chill	cell
5. shape	chop	safe
6. sip	chip	ship
7. whine	shine	chin
8. thick	chick	ship
9. whale	hill	shell
10. chill	while	hail
11. shall	hall	whole
12. cloth	class	clock
13. pass	posh	path
14. truth	trunk	trust
15. bash	bench	bath
16. pick	post	pinch
17. rush	ranch	rash
18. catch	cash	cast
19. hit	hitch	hash
20. pit	pick	pitch
21. brush	brick	brass
22. ditch	dish	duck
23. smack	smash	small

2. Another form, somewhat more difficult, is to ask students to print words that either begin or end with a consonant digraph that you dictate. Use words from the lists, pages 120–121.

3. Print a set of words that begin or end with consonant digraphs on a sheet of paper or use flashcards. Students may read the list aloud individually to you. Or it might be read by a group of students, one word per student, as you take notes on who makes what errors.

Long Vowel Words with Final [e]

This can be assessed in several ways:

1. On 8½″ × 11″ paper, print any ten of the 20 sets of words shown below—a target word and two alternatives—and duplicate for each student. Ask students to circle the word you read. (Omit underlining on student copies.)

Select sets of words so that the target words you read include [a], [i], [o], and [u], short and long vowel words.

1.	cup	<u>cube</u>	cub
2.	<u>cut</u>	cat	cute
3.	tug	<u>tube</u>	tub
4.	fit	<u>fade</u>	fad
5.	tame	tum	<u>tam</u>
6.	pale	<u>pal</u>	pill
7.	<u>rid</u>	red	ride
8.	wine	<u>win</u>	won
9.	shin	shone	<u>shine</u>
10.	<u>code</u>	cod	cud
11.	glib	glob	<u>globe</u>
12.	note	net	<u>not</u>
13.	tip	<u>tap</u>	tape
14.	<u>plan</u>	plane	place
15.	sled	<u>slide</u>	slid
16.	<u>dim</u>	dome	dime
17.	rod	red	<u>rode</u>
18.	<u>cone</u>	con	cane
19.	hag	huge	<u>hug</u>
20.	<u>plume</u>	plum	plate

2. Another form, somewhat more difficult, is to ask students to print CVC and CVC[e] words that you dictate.

3. Or you might duplicate a set of CVC and CVC[e] words, in random order. Students may read the list aloud individually to you. A longer list may be read by a group of students, one word per student, as you take notes on who makes what errors. Flash cards can be made and used in the same manner.

Vowels Followed by [r]

This can be assessed in several ways:

1. On 8½″ × 11″ paper, print any ten of the following eighteen sets of words—a target word and two alternatives—and duplicate for each student. Ask students to circle the word you read. (Do not underline the target words on the student copies.)

Target words should be [ar], [er], [ir], [or], or [ur] words.

1.	shark	shack	shirt
2.	jar	gem	germ
3.	skate	skirt	scarf
4.	perk	pork	poke
5.	time	term	tore
6.	surf	sort	safe
7.	sport	spark	spike
8.	clerk	clock	click
9.	strike	stir	store
10.	float	flirt	fort
11.	squirt	score	scar
12.	cream	corn	curl
13.	mike	make	mark
14.	farm	fern	fame
15.	girl	gale	gill
16.	short	shirt	sheet
17.	tar	turn	tune
18.	yarn	whirl	wore

2. Another way to assess would be to print a set of eight V[r] words on the board from the sentences below. Pass out paper and after students print their names, have them number 1 to 8 down their pages. Then read aloud a sentence, leaving out the V[r] word. Tell students they are to choose the word to fit the sentence (or description) and print it on their papers beside number 1. Proceed similarly with sentences for numbers 2–8.

Following is a set of eighteen sentences (or descriptions) as suggestions. Students do not see the sentences that you read to them—only a set of word choices is on the board.

1. On its trunk and branches, every tree has a layer of bark.
2. When it is not light out, it is dark.
3. We buy jelly and pickles in a jar.
4. A yellow vegetable with tiny kernels is corn.
5. A colt is a baby horse.
6. Rose bushes often have thorns.

7. When asleep, some people <u>snore</u>.
8. You buy groceries at the <u>store</u>.
9. The seeds of an apple are in its <u>core</u>.
10. Many cows together are called a <u>herd</u>.
11. The school year usually has four <u>terms</u>.
12. The yellow bird was swinging on its <u>perch</u>.
13. A robin is a red-breasted <u>bird</u>.
14. With his jeans he wore a cotton <u>shirt</u>.
15. After the second inning comes the <u>third</u>.
16. A match can be used to make paper <u>burn</u>.
17. Cars have to be careful on bad <u>curves</u>.
18. A lady's pocketbook is called a <u>purse</u>.

Scoring:

Use your judgment about the number of items to test and the number correct to consider adequate. However, more than two or three incorrect out of ten usually indicates that further teaching and practice may be necessary.

Vowel Digraphs

The common vowel digraphs that stand for the long vowel sounds, [ai], [ay], [ee], [ea], and [oa], should probably be assessed before you teach the variant vowel digraphs and diphthongs. The formats suggested below may be used for both sets, and the examples given are divided—one set for the common long vowels and one for the other vowel digraphs and diphthongs. Use the word lists, pages 132–133 and 135–136, to create other items and sentences.

Vowel digraphs may be assessed in several ways. Following are some suggestions.

1. You might duplicate, for each student, a paper with ten sets of words—a target word and two alternatives. (Do not underline target words on student copies.) Students are to circle the words you read.

Following are two lists with sets of words you may wish to choose from:

Common Long Vowels

1. <u>mail</u>	meal	mile
2. jeep	goal	<u>jail</u>
3. trim	tree	<u>train</u>
4. deed	<u>day</u>	deal
5. trap	<u>tray</u>	treat
6. <u>stay</u>	steal	steel

7.	bay	<u>bee</u>	by
8.	fade	foal	<u>feed</u>
9.	<u>cheek</u>	check	chain
10.	float	<u>flea</u>	flat
11.	<u>deal</u>	dale	dome
12.	<u>clean</u>	clan	claim
13.	tad	<u>toad</u>	tail
14.	ketch	catch	<u>coach</u>
15.	gain	gale	<u>goal</u>

Other Vowel Digraphs and Diphthongs

1.	cob	<u>coin</u>	cow
2.	paint	pint	<u>point</u>
3.	jaw	jay	<u>joy</u>
4.	tail	<u>toy</u>	tea
5.	<u>die</u>	day	dead
6.	tea	<u>tie</u>	team
7.	<u>brief</u>	broth	brake
8.	<u>thief</u>	tooth	thread
9.	broil	<u>bowl</u>	pool
10.	sheet	shout	<u>show</u>
11.	creed	<u>crowd</u>	cried
12.	<u>plow</u>	plea	ply
13.	creek	crick	<u>crook</u>
14.	shack	shake	<u>shook</u>
15.	<u>cool</u>	coil	cloud
16.	<u>room</u>	roam	ream
17.	fail	<u>fault</u>	fool
18.	pouch	piece	<u>pause</u>
19.	drew	<u>draw</u>	drain
20.	shell	<u>shawl</u>	shame
21.	<u>crew</u>	cry	caw
22.	stay	straw	<u>stew</u>
23.	coach	cinch	<u>couch</u>
24.	<u>proud</u>	pride	pray
25.	deep	<u>deaf</u>	food
26.	swat	sweet	<u>sweat</u>

2. Print ten vowel digraph words on the board from the following sentences. Pass out paper and after students print their names, have them number 1 to 10 down their papers. Then read aloud the first sentence, <u>leaving out the vowel digraph word</u>. Tell students they are to choose the word to fit the sentence (or description) and print it on their papers beside number 1. Proceed similarly for numbers 2–10.

Following are sets of sentences (or descriptions) as suggestions. Students do not see the sentences that you read to them—only the word choices are on the board.

Common Long Vowels

1. Magazines, letters, and postcards may come in the <u>mail</u>.
2. Striking your thumb with a hammer causes a lot of <u>pain</u>.
3. Dark clouds often appear just before the <u>rain</u>.
4. Cows and sheep like to eat <u>hay</u>.
5. Pottery can be made from <u>clay</u>.
6. When carrying dishes, we may make use of a <u>tray</u>.
7. If you want lettuce to grow, you plant lettuce <u>seeds</u>.
8. When you cry, a tear might run down your <u>cheek</u>.
9. Most kings are married to a <u>queen</u>.
10. Highways, roads, and lanes are often called <u>streets</u>.
11. If you are hurt, you want your sores to <u>heal</u>.
12. Many people like to add this to their coffee: <u>cream</u>.
13. One of the grains used in making bread is <u>wheat</u>.
14. Sometimes people refer to frogs as <u>toads</u>.
15. If you borrow a book from the library, it is on <u>loan</u>.
16. To get clean, you may want to use water and plenty of <u>soap</u>.

Other Vowel Digraphs and Diphthongs

1. You plant seeds in dirt, or <u>soil</u>.
2. Leaving milk out of the refrigerator will cause it to <u>spoil</u>.
3. Children are sometimes called girls and <u>boys</u>.
4. Blueberries, apples, and cherries all make good <u>pie</u>.
5. Grasses, flowers, and rocks may be found in the <u>field</u>.
6. The fire department needs a new <u>chief</u>.
7. This large black bird says, "Caw": <u>crow</u>.
8. If it is cold enough, rather than rain we will have <u>snow</u>.
9. This is a bright, cheery color: <u>yellow</u>.
10. This person is dressed for fun in the circus: <u>clown</u>.
11. A long dress worn to a fancy ball is called a <u>gown</u>.
12. A small stream or running water in the woods is called a <u>brook</u>.
13. You might catch a fish with a worm on a <u>hook</u>.
14. If it is very wet outside, you might want to wear your <u>boots</u>.
15. At night, we can see many stars and the <u>moon</u>.
16. Hammers, wrenches, screwdrivers, and pliers are called <u>tools</u>.
17. This usually goes under a cup: <u>saucer</u>.
18. If a baby is hungry or hurt, he or she will cry very loudly, or <u>bawl</u>.
19. Each of the new kittens had four black and white <u>paws</u>.

20. Sometimes when you are tired, you <u>yawn</u>.
21. This is what you do when you put gum in your mouth: <u>chew</u>.
22. This is what a kitten or cat will do to get your attention: <u>mew</u>.
23. A liquid food made by boiling meat or vegetables is <u>soup</u>.
24. People live in these: <u>houses</u>.
25. This is the direction that is opposite of north: <u>south</u>.

3. Prepare lists of words or flashcards from the word lists of vowel digraphs, beginning on page 130, and follow the procedures for having students read as suggested for other phonic elements.

Since the words are not in context, praise efforts when students give an alternate reading of a word that includes an acceptable sound for the vowel digraph. For instance, reading "spreed" for *spread* should be responded to by acknowledging that [ea] often stands for long [e], but not in the word *spread*. Ask the student to try another sound for [ea] to see if he or she can get a known word.

Dictation is probably not a good assessment tool for vowel digraphs unless you are willing to allow for variant spellings that represent the correct vowel sounds but are not the accepted spelling of the dictated word. For instance, if the target word is *steed*, and the student prints *stead*, it would be useful to take the time to acknowledge to him or her that [ea] is one way of spelling the long [e] sound, but it is not the way it is spelled in the word *steed*. Ask the student for another long [e] spelling for the word.

Syllabication

Syllabication is useful in helping a student to decide whether a vowel should be short or long. Assessment might, therefore, focus on having students read two-syllable words with the following patterns: CVC/CVC (where the division between the vowels indicates that the first vowel is short); CV/C[le] (where the division before the C[le] indicates that the first vowel is long, as in *table*); and CVC/C[le] (where the division before the C[le] indicates that the first vowel is short, as in *rattle*).

Probably the best way to assess syllabication is to have students read various polysyllabic words orally—from two to three and four syllables, with different prefixes and suffixes. The teacher assesses knowledge and skill qualitatively and judges whether additional instruction and practice are needed.

Word Patterns

We would suggest that words containing the following patterns be selected from the appropriate word lists on pages 147–148: [ild] as in *child*, [ind] as in *kind*, [igh] as in *fight*, [olt] as in *colt*, [old] as in *cold*, [ost] as in *most*, and [all] and [alt] as in *fall* and *salt*. Printing these words as a list or on flashcards and asking individuals or small groups of students to read them aloud will indicate whether they have learned the patterns.

Phonics Checklist

You can use this checklist (page 104) to keep a record of each student's progress. As an element is learned, check it off on the list.

Suggestions for Providing Remedial Instruction

Following each assessment, we suggest that you pay particular attention to those students who score "inadequately." If you think the score or scores underestimate what the student can do, temper the scores with your own judgment. If, however, the inadequate scores agree with your judgment, additional instruction should be undertaken as early as possible. This can be done on a one-to-one basis or in groups of two, three, or more students who need similar instruction. You should realize that more time will be needed for these students.

The additional instruction, in most cases, can be a review of the lesson taught originally, using different words from the word lists in the Appendix. The emphasis should be on presenting the material orally and having students respond orally. This will provide opportunities for much needed practice and for immediate feedback. You will know right away whether the difficulty persists or some progress is being made. It is essential, also, that the phonic elements and generalizations being reviewed are applied to new words in isolation, in phrases and sentences, and in stories. Students should also write the words from dictation.

In addition, you should be on the lookout for errors that reveal weaknesses in phonic elements or generalizations taught earlier. For example, if the student missed writing the word *cute* on an assessment designed to determine knowledge of the long vowel [u] with a final [e], he or she might have failed the item because of uncertain knowledge of the consonants [c] or [t]. Then, a quick review of the forgotten element or generalization is in order.

It is important to realize that some of your students—at all levels of ability and background—may have extreme difficulty learning phonics. Even some very able children may find phonics very difficult. As noted earlier (see chapter 5, page 29), it has been estimated that from ten percent to as much as twenty percent of the population has such difficulty.[1] Fortunately, available research and experience

Phonics Checklist

Consonants

	Initial	Final
s		
m		
r		
t		
b		
f		
n		
p		
d		
h		
c /k/		
g /g/		
j		
l		
k		
v		
w		
z		
c /s/		
g /j/		
qu		
y		

	Final Only
ck	
x	
ss	
ll	
tt	
ff	
bb	
dd	
pp	

Short Vowels

CVC words

a	
e	
i	
o	
u	

Blends

	Initial
bl	
cl	
fl	
pl	
br	
dr	
gr	
tr	
cr	
fr	
pr	
gl	
sl	
sn	
sp	
st	
sw	
sc	
sk	

	Final
ft	
lp	
mp	
nd	
nk	
nt	
pt	
sk	
sp	
st	

Consonant Digraphs

sh	
ch	
th	
wh	
ph	

Long Vowels

CVCe words

a	
e	
i	
o	
u	

y as a Vowel

/e/ (bunny)	
/i/ (by)	

Vowels followed by r

ar	
or	
er	
ir	
ur	

Silent Letters

Initial		Final	
kn		-tch	
wr		-dge	
gh		-gh	
sc		-lk	
gn			

Vowel Digraphs

ai (paid)	
ay (pay)	
oa (boat)	
ee (tree)	
oe (toe)	
oi (join)	
oy (joy)	
ew (chew)	
ou (cloud)	
ou (soup)	
au (haul)	
aw (saw)	
ea (preach)	
ea (deaf)	

Vowel digraphs, cont.

ow (crow)	
ow (cow)	
oo (boot)	
oo (hook)	
ie (pie)	
ie (thief)	
ey (they)	
ey (valley)	
ei (ceiling)	
ui (build)	
ui (fruit)	

Prefixes

dis	
un	
re	
im	
in	
mis	
pre	

Suffixes

-ful	
-ly	
-less	
-ness	
-able	
-ible	
-ion	
-ment	
-er	
-or	
-en	

Vowels in Spelling Patterns

ind (bind)	
ild (wild)	
igh (high)	
old (cold)	
olt (colt)	
ost (host)	
ost (cost)	

also find that with good instruction these students do learn to read, although it may take them longer. Much of their improvement depends on the teacher's knowledge of and skill with phonics now.[2]

Those who make slower progress need to be stimulated as much as those making faster progress. Their lessons should be as vigorous and lively as for all students.

In general, we suggest that when you use worksheets, you give explanations and instructions orally, thus assuring that the students know what to do. Also, check the exercises to be sure they have been done properly. An oral review of the completed page (particularly of incorrect responses) will often reveal why a student made the error. It is important that the worksheet is relevant to what you are presently teaching. Assigning workbook pages unrelated to the current instruction is usually not helpful.

The students who need extra help, as well as those who make good progress, need much encouragement and confirmation from you. They need to know that they are learning the material and making progress. This can be done best by providing instruction that is "just right" in difficulty—not too hard and not too easy. (The order of the phonic elements in Chapter 7, Part 1 is designed to go from easy to hard.) In addition, we recommend that you recognize a student's success even if it is only for part of the task. Thus, if he or she says *can* instead of *cat*, it is helpful to say, "That is good, you have most of it right. Now look at the last letter."

For students who progress very slowly, particularly at the beginning, we suggest that faster progress can be made if you focus first on their strengths in learning how to read. The following section contains suggestions for tapping these strengths, and describes other approaches for learning word recognition and phonics.

Alternative Approaches for Students Having Difficulty with Phonics*

For those students who have great difficulty learning phonics from the very beginning, we suggest using one or more of the following approaches to word recognition and phonics—visual, visual-motor,

*We acknowledge the seminal work of Florence G. Roswell for this section on alternative approaches. See in this connection her books—Florence G. Roswell and Gladys Natchez, *Reading Disability: A Human Approach to Evaluation and Treatment of Reading and Writing Difficulties,* 4th ed. (New York: Basic Books, 1989), and Florence G. Roswell and Jeanne S. Chall, *Creating Successful Readers: A Practical Guide to Testing and Teaching at All Levels* (Chicago: Riverside, 1994).

kinesthetic, and linguistic patterns. As the student learns to recognize words by these approaches, a phonic blending approach should be tried again (see page 75).

If the students fail to progress with phonics and with other aspects of reading, we suggest that you consult a reading specialist.

Visual Approach

With a visual approach, students are taught to read words by associating them with pictures. Subsequently they read these words in phrases and short sentences. Words thus learned may then be used to illustrate phonic elements and generalizations and to help in demonstrating auditory blending or other aspects of phonemic awareness.

Sight Words

Create or obtain cards that show a word by itself on one side and the word with a picture that represents that word on the other side. Select words for unambiguous objects and actions that are familiar and meaningful to the student, such as *horse, dog, cat, girl, man, boy, jump, run,* and *sit.* Show the student the words on the non-illustrated sides of the cards to determine those that may be known already. Then choose three to five of those that the student does not know and proceed to teach them as follows:

Using the illustrated side of these three to five noun cards, say to the student, "This is a picture of a _____ [e.g., *horse*]. Do you see the word under the picture? The word is *horse.* This is a picture of a horse and the word under it is *horse.*" Additional noun cards are introduced in a similar way.

Then proceed with each card: "Now take a good look at the word under the picture and say each word as you look at the word and its picture. Look at each word carefully and then turn the picture over and study the word alone. You may study each word as long as you like by looking at it with the picture and then on the other side of the card where the word stands by itself. When you think you know these words [each lesson should teach approximately three to five new words], tell me. Then you can shuffle the cards and read the words without the pictures." After several nouns are learned, add action verbs, being sure the written word is understood as the pictured action.

When the student learns ten to twelve words, teach the words *can* and *and.* Present the words in sentences such as:

The dog can run.

The dog can jump.

The dog can run and jump.

As soon as the student begins to learn words by connecting them with pictures, introduce a simple illustrated reader at a preprimer level, one that introduces new words very slowly so that the chances of success are favorable. The level of difficulty of the stories should be increased gradually as the student's ability to recall the words learned increases, and he or she can read them accurately in connected text.

Encourage the student to illustrate phrases or sentences and also create and write his or her own sentences. The known words can then be used, gradually, to introduce phonics—initial consonant sounds first and then short vowels in simple consonant-vowel-consonant (CVC) words.

Predictable Stories

Many interesting children's books contain words and phrases that are repeated many times throughout the book. You can guide students through repeated oral readings of these books. Pairs of students can also reread them together. The recurring words and phrases and strong picture clues help the student identify the words. Follow these rereadings with a focus on identifying the high frequency words in isolation or in short phrases. Eventually, these same words can be used to teach the phonic elements and generalizations and to encourage phonic blending.

Visual-Motor Approach

Sometimes adding a "motor" component to the teaching of words is helpful to students having difficulty. For a visual-motor approach the student is given a card with one word printed on it and told, "Close your eyes and try to see the word. Open your eyes and look at the word again. What is the word?" This may be done several times, and then the student is asked to cover the word and write it from memory. The written word is compared to the word on the card, and the procedure is repeated if a mistake has been made. No erasures are permitted, and trials continue until the word is written accurately. Then the student writes it several more times for practice, each time from memory. Another word is introduced and the same procedure is followed. After three or four words are mastered, all are reviewed.

Kinesthetic Approach

Another approach useful for those who have difficulty with the visual and visual-motor approaches is the kinesthetic. The student is asked to select a word he or she wishes to learn. The word is printed on paper in fairly large letters by the teacher, and the student traces it with his or her index finger as he or she simultaneously pronounces the word. The word is traced again, and the student pronounces it. Then the student is asked to write the word without referring to the model. If the student has difficulty, the procedure continues—tracing and saying the word until it can be written without looking at the original.

Words learned in this manner are then used in phrases, sentences, and stories. Eventually words can be learned without the tracing component, and simple reading texts are introduced (as for the sight approach above). The learned words are used in teaching phonic elements and generalizations and in practicing phonic blending.

Linguistic Patterns (Word Families or Spelling Patterns)

Another approach that is easier to learn than phonic blending is that of linguistic patterns. Sets of words in word families, i.e., simple CVC rhyming words such as *cap, lap, map, nap, sap, tap,* or *bat, cat, hat, mat, fat, pat, sat* are built by substituting different beginning consonants. Chapter 7, Part 2, page 71 offers some suggestions for teaching initial consonants, and page 73 offers suggestions for teaching the technique of initial consonant substitution. For example, you might write [at] on the board; add [b] and ask for the word; add [c] and ask for the word; add [h] and ask for the word, etc.

Also, ask students which consonants should be added to form the word you say. For instance, begin by writing [at] on the board and ask students what letter you should add to form the word *bat;* then the word *cat;* etc.

Be sure the student practices reading these words orally in isolation and in sentences (see below) and can write them.

> *That cat has a hat.*
>
> *Pat the cat.*
>
> *The hat is on the rat.*
>
> *The rat is on the mat.*
>
> *The rat has a bat.*
>
> *The cat can bat the rat.*

Then introduce another pattern such as [an] as in *ran, can, fan,* etc. We suggest that you do not stay too long with any one pattern. After one pattern is learned, move on to another.

Continue to build the sets of words with simple CVC patterns, and introduce function words such as *the, and, of,* as needed. Guide the students in writing and reading the words. With only a few patterns and several function words, students can create, read, write, and illustrate real sentences and "silly sentences." For example, [at], [ig], [an], [it], and [ad] words can be used to build the following sentences:

The rat sat on a big can.

The pig had a big hat.

Dad had a wig.

Can a fan jig?

The man can sit in the van.

Dan had a tan cat.

The cat ran and the sad pig sat.

This approach can be used as an introduction to phonic blending as soon as it is feasible. From time to time as you are working with a student on linguistic patterns, try auditory blending to determine whether the student is ready to learn phonic blending. Chapter 7, Part 2, page 75 gives that procedure in detail. In effect, you will separate the sounds in words and ask the student to tell you what the word is. If the student can identify six out of nine simple CVC words you pronounce, you should be able to proceed to the phonic blending approach.

Auditory blending is described as a prerequisite skill in Chapter 2, page 11, but you should be aware that some students continue to have great difficulty with it even after they have learned many words. These students should continue with a modified phonic approach (see below).

Modified Phonic Blending Approach[3]

The modified phonic blending approach is recommended for students who succeed with the linguistic patterns but who are still unable to blend sounds auditorily. They, therefore, should not proceed to phonic blending. This modified phonic approach relies on both visual and auditory methods and on much reinforcement through writing. It does not rely on blending.

Suggestions for this approach follow. Say, "Now that you have learned to read many new words by changing the beginning letters, I'm going to show you how to read new words by changing the last letters as well as the beginning letters. First you will write words you already know. Then you'll use this knowledge to read and write new words. As I say the words to you, write them in a column, one word beneath the other. There will be three columns: one on the left side, one in the middle, and one on the right side. In the first column write the word *cat*; now under *cat* write *rat* and under *rat* write *mat*." Look at the student's page and correct and explain any errors. Review any phonic elements that were incorrect.

"Now in the second column," (point) "the first word to write is *can*, below that write *ran*, and below that write *man*. Now in the column over here," (point to the column on the right) "the first word to write is *cap*; write the word *rap* under *cap*, and under *rap* write *map*." Have the student read the words, column by column, assisting when necessary and correcting any misreading. Then have him or her read the words going across the page; the top line, the middle line, and the bottom line. Point out to the student that when reading across the page, he or she is reading words where the last letter was changed.

Then say, "Now write these words in a list. I'll say each word slowly." Pronounce consonants clearly. Elongate vowel sounds. "It will help you to write the words correctly if you say each one slowly as you write it. Write *cat, can, cap, rat, ran, rap, mat, man, map*." Dictate words one at a time. "Now read the words you wrote. You see that today you learned still another way of extending your reading vocabulary by reading and writing words where the last letter is changed. Did you notice as you read the words that all of them had the short [a] vowel sound in the middle? It's the first sound you hear when you say the word *apple*. Listen for the short [a] sound as I say these words: *cat, man, cap, rat, fan*." (Elongate the short [a] sound as you say the words.) "Here's a picture of an apple to help you remember the short [a] sound."

Proceed slowly. After the student grasps the idea of changing only the final consonant (the first consonant and vowel remain the same), present words in mixed order, changing both initial and final consonants (see below).

Then say, "Let's try some more words, only this time I'm going to ask you to write words where both the beginning and last letters are changed. Again, I'll say each word slowly and you say each one slowly to yourself as you write it: *sap, tag, mad, can, jam, sad, bag*. Now read what you wrote." Practice in saying and writing words simultaneously reinforces learning.

The next step is having students write the words learned in phrases: *the sad man, pat the cat, the tan bag*, and so on.

When students have mastered writing words and phrases with the short [a] vowel sound, say, "Now that you've learned to write and read words with the short [a] vowel sound, I'm going to teach you other short vowel sounds. There are four more, and I'll teach them one at a time." See pages 113-114 for suggested words to help create meaningful phrases.

The additional vowels are taught in a similar manner to the short [a] vowel sound. The suggested sequence is [a], [o], [i], [u], [e]. After you teach each vowel, dictate words that include all previously taught vowels in mixed order.

To summarize the modified phonic blending approach: (1) The students write the words dictated in vertical columns, where only the initial consonant is changed; (2) The student reads the words written in the vertical column; (3) The student reads the words across the page where the initial consonant is constant but the final consonant is changed; (4) The teacher calls attention to the short vowel sound in the words just read and associates the vowel sounds with a picture; (5) The teacher dictates words where initial and final consonants are interchanged; (6) Vowel sounds previously taught are reviewed through writing words from dictation in mixed order; and (7) Phrases containing words taught are written from dictation.

The students always read words or phrases after writing them. The pace at which these exercises are presented will depend on the student's ability to grasp instruction, including writing to reinforce reading. The exercises can be shortened for those students who catch on to the method quickly and extended for those who catch on slowly. To give practice in applying what they learn in the exercise, and to maintain students' interest in reading, it is suggested that the exercises be kept brief and be followed by reading appealing stories, rhymes, or riddles.

When students show ability to read CVC words containing all short vowel sounds using the modified phonic approach, go on to the regular phonic blending approach. (See Chapter 5, page 31, and Chapter 7, Part 2, pages 75–76 for a discussion of the phonic blending approach and suggestions for teaching it.) Then teach the rule of silent [e] and the rest of the phonic elements and generalizations found in Part 1 of this chapter.

Additional Suggestions for Remedial Teaching

While some students may find it easier at the beginning to use visual methods for recognizing words, they can learn phonic elements and procedures at the same time when appropriate instruction is given. Also, as students progress in word recognition and phonics, whether their progress is fast or slow, they should be reading connected text that is not too difficult for them.

Since students who have difficulty are easily discouraged, they need encouragement. And yet, when students and teacher persist, they do ultimately learn phonics well enough to be able to use it in their reading. To achieve this, it is usually not necessary to devote all reading time to phonics. Instead, it can usually be done with short practice periods of five to ten minutes per day. In addition, as noted earlier, the students should keep reading books of appropriate difficulty that interest them and that provide practice in using their growing knowledge and skills in phonics.

Phonics must not be made to carry the whole burden of reading instruction, especially if students have difficulty with it. Although research and experience have demonstrated again and again that phonic knowledge and skill are essential for learning to read, and that they speed up learning to read, there is also considerable evidence that reading development depends on wide reading of connected text, the development of fluency, and the growth of vocabulary, knowledge, and reasoning.

Thus, it is wise for all students, even those having extreme difficulty with phonics, to read books they find interesting, learn the meanings of ever more difficult words, and continue to acquire knowledge. As they become more proficient in phonics and word recognition, they will develop greater fluency and understand increasingly challenging and mature reading matter.

Notes

1. Louise Spear-Swerling and Robert J. Sternberg, *Off Track: When poor readers become "learning disabled"* (Boulder, CO: Westview Press, 1996).

2. John B. Carroll, "Thoughts on reading and phonics" (paper presented at the meeting of the National Conference on Research in English, Atlanta, GA, May 9, 1990).

3. The modified phonic blending approach was developed by Florence Roswell. Our section on it is taken from Florence G. Roswell and Jeanne S. Chall, *Creating Successful Readers: A Practical Guide to Testing and Teaching at All Levels* (Chicago: Riverside, 1994).

Appendix

Short Vowel Words
With Single Consonants—CVC

a		e	
cab	can	web	bet
jab	fan	___	get
tab	man		jet
	pan	bed	let
___	ran	fed	met
	tan	led	net
bad		red	pet
dad			set
had	___	___	vet
lad	cap		
mad	lap	leg	wet
pad	map	peg	yet
sad	nap		
___	rap	___	den
	tap	sap	
bag		hen	
rag		men	
tag	___	pen	
wag	gas	ten	
___	___	___	
pal	bat	pep	
	cat		
___	fat	___	
	hat		
dam	mat	yes	
ham	pat		
jam	rat	___	
ram	sat		
tam	vat		
___			

Short Vowel Words
With Single Consonants—CVC, *cont.*

i		o	u	
bib	dip	cob	cub	but
fib	hip	job	rub	cut
rib	lip	mob	sub	hut
___	nip	rob	tub	nut
	rip	sob	___	
bid	sip	___		
did	tip		bud	
hid	zip	fog	mud	
kid	___	hog	___	
lid		jog		
rid	bit	log	bug	
___	fit	___	dug	
	hit		hug	
big	kit	mom	jug	
dig	lit	___	mug	
fig	pit		rug	
jig	quit	cop	tug	
pig	sit	hop	___	
rig		pop		
wig		top	gum	
___		___	hum	
			sum	
dim		cot	___	
him		dot		
rim		got	bun	
___		hot	fun	
		lot	gun	
fin		not	run	
pin		pot	sun	
sin		rot	___	
tin		___	cup	
win			pup	
		box	___	
		fox	bus	
			___	

Short Vowel Words

With Two-Letter Initial and/or Final Consonant Blends— CCVC, CVCC, and CCVCC

a		e	
ask	lamp	bend	step
band	land	bent	swept
bank	last	best	tent
blank	mask	bled	test
blast	mast	blend	wept
brag	past	crept	west
brat	plan	crest	
brand	plank	dent	
cast	plant	desk	
clam	prank	end	
clamp	raft	felt	
clap	ramp	fled	
crab	sand	help	
damp	sank	kept	
drag	scab	left	
drank	scat	lent	
fast	slam	melt	
flag	slant	mend	
flap	slap	nest	
flat	snap	pest	
glad	spank	rest	
grab	stab	self	
grand	stand	sent	
grant	swam	sled	
hand	tank	slept	
	task	sped	
	tramp	spend	
	trap	spent	
	vast		

From *Teaching and Assessing Phonics*, by Jeanne S. Chall and Helen M. Popp.

Short Vowel Words
With Two-Letter Initial and/or Final Consonant Blends—
CCVC, CVCC, and CCVCC, *cont.*

i		o
blink	ship	blob
brim	sift	blond
brisk	silk	blot
clip	sink	bond
crib	skid	clog
crisp	skim	clop
disk	skin	clot
drift	skip	crop
drink	slid	drop
drip	slim	flop
film	slip	frog
fist	slit	glob
flip	snip	honk
frisk	spin	plop
gift	spit	plot
grim	stilt	pond
grin	stink	prod
grip	swift	prop
hint	swim	romp
ink	tilt	slop
lift	tint	slot
limp	trim	smog
link	trip	snob
list	twig	soft
mink	twin	spot
mist	twist	stop
pink	wilt	trot
print	wind	
rink	wink	
risk	wisp	

Short Vowel Words

With Two-Letter Initial and/or Final Consonant Blends— CCVC, CVCC, and CCVCC, *cont.*

u

bulb	jump
bulk	lump
bump	must
bunk	plug
bunt	plum
bust	plump
club	plus
clump	pump
clunk	rust
crust	skunk
dusk	slug
drug	slum
drum	slump
drunk	smug
dump	snug
dunk	spun
dusk	stump
dust	stun
flunk	stunt
glum	sunk
grub	swum
grunt	trunk
gulf	trust
gulp	tusk
gust	
hulk	
hump	
hunk	
hunt	
husk	

Short Vowel Words
With Three-Letter Consonant Blends—CCCVC and CCCVCC

scr	spl		spr	str
scrap	splash		sprang	strand
scrub	split		sprig	strap
			spring	stress
			sprint	string
			sprung	strip
				strong
				struck
				strum
				strung
				strut

Short Vowel Words
With Final Geminate Consonants and [ck]

a	e	i	o	u
staff	egg	cliff	block	bluff
bass	bell	sniff	clock	cuff
class	cell	stiff	dock	gruff
glass	fell	bill	flock	puff
pass	sell	drill	lock	scuff
jazz	smell	fill	lock	stuff
——	spell	gill	rock	dull
back	swell	grill	sock	gull
black	tell	hill	stock	hull
clack	well	ill		skull
crack	yell	kill		fuss
lack	bless	mill		muss
pack	dress	pill		buzz
rack	less	skill		fuzz
sack	mess	spill		——
snack	press	still		buck
stack	——	till		cluck
tack	deck	will		duck
track	neck	hiss		luck
	peck	kiss		puck
	speck	miss		suck
		——		stuck
		brick		struck
		click		tuck
		kick		truck
		lick		
		pick		
		sick		
		slick		
		stick		
		tick		
		trick		

Short Vowel Words
With Initial Consonant Digraphs

ch	sh	th	wh
champ	shack	thank	whack
chant	shaft	theft	wham
chap	shell	thick	when
chat	shed	thin	which
check	shelf	thing	whiff
chess	shell	think	whip
chest	shift	thud	whisk
chick	shin	thump	whiz
chill	ship		
chimp	shock	___	
chin	shop	than	
chip	shot	that	
chop	shut	them	
chuck		then	
chug		this	
chum		thus	
chunk			

Short Vowel Words
With Final Consonant Digraphs and [tch]

-ch	-sh	-th	-tch
branch	cash	bath	batch
ranch	clash	math	catch
bench	crash	path	hatch
clench	dash	tenth	latch
drench	flash	with	match
trench	mash		patch
clinch	rash		scratch
rich	sash		snatch
finch	smash		ditch
flinch	trash		hitch
inch	fresh		itch
pinch	dish		pitch
much	fish		stitch
such	wish		switch
bunch	blush		twitch
crunch	brush		
hunch	crush		
lunch	flush		
munch	gush		
punch	hush		
	mush		
	rush		
	slush		

Alternate Consonant Sounds
Soft [c] and [g] Words

ceiling	general
celebrate	gentle
cell	gentleman
cellar	geography
cent	gelatin
center	gem
cereal	generous
cigarette	genius
circle	gently
circus	geometry
citizen	germ
city	gesture
cease	giant
cedar	gin
celery	ginger
cement	gingerbread
cemetery	giraffe
census	gym
central	gypsy
century	
certain	
certificate	
cider	
cigar	
cinder	
cinnamon	
civic	
civil	
civilize	
cyclone	
cycle	

Long Vowel Words: With Final Silent [e]
One-Syllable Words—CVC[e]

	a			i	
face	cage	cape	bribe	file	bite
grace	page	grape	tribe	mile	kite
lace	rage	scrape	—	pile	white
pace	stage	shape	dice	smile	write
place	wage	tape	lice	tile	—
race	—	—	mice	while	dive
space	gale	base	nice	—	drive
trace	male	case	price	chime	five
—	pale	chase	rice	crime	hive
blade	sale	vase	slice	dime	live
fade	tale	—	spice	lime	
grade	scale	crate	twice	slime	
made	stale	date	—	time	
shade	whale	fate	bride	—	
spade	—	gate	glide	dine	
trade	blame	grate	hide	fine	
wade	came	hate	pride	line	
—	fame	late	ride	mine	
bake	flame	mate	side	nine	
brake	frame	plate	slide	pine	
cake	game	rate	stride	shine	
fake	lame	skate	tide	spine	
flake	name	state	wide	swine	
lake	same	—	—	twine	
make	shame	brave	life	vine	
rake	tame	cave	wife	wine	
sake	—	gave	—	—	
shake	cane	grave	bike	gripe	
snake	crane	save	dike	pipe	
stake	lane	shave	hike	ripe	
take	mane	slave	like	stripe	
wake	pane	wave	spike	wipe	
—	plane		strike	—	
	vane		—	rise	
				wise	

Long Vowel Words: With Final Silent [e]
One-Syllable Words—CVC[e], *cont.*

o

globe	hole	hope
robe	mole	rope
—	pole	slope
code	stole	—
rode	whole	
—	—	chose
broke	dome	close
choke	home	hose
joke	—	nose
poke	bone	rose
smoke	cone	those
spoke	lone	—
stroke	stone	note
woke	tone	vote
—	zone	—
	—	cove
		drove
		grove
		stove

u

cube	tube
mule	crude
yule	dude
fuse	rude
use	duke
cute	rule
—	plume
	dune
	June
	prune
	tune
	flute

Contrasting Short and Long Vowel Words—
CVC and CVC[e]

a		i		o	
grad	grade	hid	hide	glob	globe
mad	made	rid	ride	rob	robe
pal	pale	slid	slide	cod	code
tam	tame	dim	dime	rod	rode
can	cane	slim	slime	hop	hope
man	mane	fin	fine	slop	slope
pan	pane	pin	pine	not	note
plan	plane	shin	shine		
van	vane	spin	spine		
cap	cape	twin	twine	cub	cube
scrap	scrape	win	wine	us	use
tap	tape	grip	gripe	cut	cute
fat	fate	rip	ripe	tub	tube
hat	hate	strip	stripe	plum	plume
mat	mate	bit	bite		
rat	rate	kit	kite		

Long Vowels at the End of Words

(See also two-syllable words with single medial consonant on page 141.)

e	i	o
be	hi	go
he		ho
me		lo
she		no
we		so

[y] as a Vowel

Long [i]	Long [e]	
by	angry	hungry
cry	army	hurry
dry	berry	jelly
fly	bunny	jolly
fry	candy	muddy
my	carry	mommy
pry	cherry	mummy
shy	clumsy	party
sky	daddy	penny
sly	dizzy	plenty
spy	easy	pretty
try	empty	puppy
why	fancy	sandy
	ferry	silly
	fifty	simply
	floppy	sixty
	foggy	skinny
	funny	sorry
	fuzzy	sturdy
	grizzly	sunny
	grumpy	thirty
	gully	twenty
	happy	ugly
	hobby	worry

Vowels Followed by [r]
One-Syllable Words

ar		er*	ir	ur	or
arch	part	clerk	birch	burn	born
arm	scar	fern	bird	burst	cord
art	scarf	germ	birth	church	cork
bar	shark	her	chirp	churn	corn
barb	sharp	herb	dirt	curb	for
barge	smart	herd	fir	curl	ford
bark	snarl	jerk	firm	curse	forge
barn	spark	nerve	first	curve	fork
car	star	perch	flirt	hurl	form
card	starch	serve	girl	hurt	fort
cart	start	stern	shirt	nurse	horn
carve	starve	term	skirt	purse	horse
charge	tar		smirk	surf	lord
charm	tarp		squirm	turn	morn
chart	tart		squirt	urge	north
dark	yard		stir		or
dart	yarn		swirl		porch
far			third		pork
farm			thirst		port
hard			twirl		scorch
hark			whirl		scorn
harm					short
harp					sort
harsh					sport
jar					stork
large					storm
lark					sworn
march					thorn
mark					torch
marsh					torn
park					worn

*Note that er, ir, and ur have the same sound.

Vowels Followed by [r]*

Two-Syllable Words

barber	letter
better	lobster
border	lumber
burden	market
butter	matter
carpet	monster
center	number
chapter	offer
circus	orbit
clipper	order
copper	organ
corner	pepper
current	permit
dancer	person
dinner	robber
farmer	runner
filter	serpent
finger	silver
flipper	sister
forget	slipper
garden	summer
garlic	turnip
gerbil	wander
hammer	whisker
hamster	whisper
hornet	winner
hunter	winter
ladder	

*People with different dialects may pronounce these words somewhat differently, but their pronunciation will be close enough for them to recognize the word.

Silent Consonants

d̸ge

badge
bridge
budge
dodge
fudge
grudge
judge
ledge
lodge
ridge
trudge
wedge

g̸n

gnarled
gnat
gnaw
gnu
assign
design
resign
sign

l̸k

chalk
stalk
talk
walk

k̸n

knapsack
knee
kneel
knew
knife
knight
knit
knob
knock
knot
know
knuckle

m̸b

climb
comb
crumb
dumb
lamb
limb
numb
thumb

s̸c

scent
scene
science
scissors

w̸r

wrap
wreath
wreck
wren
wrench
wrestle
wriggle
wring
wrinkle
wrist
write
wrong
wrote

Words with Inflected Endings

Plurals of Nouns Ending in [y] or [f]

y > ies

babies	pastries
berries	pennies
bunnies	ponies
candies	puppies
cavities	stories
cherries	studies
copies	
funnies	
guppies	
hobbies	
jellies	
ladies	
parties	

f or fe > ves

elves
hooves
knives
leaves
lives
loaves
scarves
selves
shelves
themselves
thieves
wives
wolves

Verb Endings: [s], [ed], and [ing]

Verb	s	ed	ing
burn	burns	burned	burning
help	helps	helped	helping
lock	locks	locked	locking
hunt	hunts	hunted	hunting
open	opens	opened	opening
bark	barks	barked	barking
rain	rains	rained	raining
clean	cleans	cleaned	cleaning
plan	plans	planned	planning
jog	jogs	jogged	jogging
hop	hops	hopped	hopping
wag	wags	wagged	wagging
trip	trips	tripped	tripping
beg	begs	begged	begging
wrap	wraps	wrapped	wrapping
rub	rubs	rubbed	rubbing

Verb Endings : [s], [ed], and [ing], *cont.*

Verb	s	ed	ing
hope	hopes	hoped	hoping
scrape	scrapes	scraped	scraping
hate	hates	hated	hating
use	uses	used	using
race	races	raced	racing
move	moves	moved	moving
save	saves	saved	saving

Vowel Digraphs
One-Syllable Words

ai = ā	ay = ā	ee = ē	
braid	bay	bee	seem
laid	clay	flee	green
maid	day	free	queen
paid	gray	three	screen
raid	hay	tree	seen
fail	jay	wee	teen
hail	lay	whee	beep
jail	may	bleed	creep
mail	pay	breed	deep
nail	play	deed	keep
pail	pray	feed	peep
rail	ray	greed	sheep
sail	say	need	sleep
snail	slay	seed	steep
tail	spray	speed	sweep
trail	stay	weed	cheer
aim	stray	beef	deer
claim	tray	cheek	steer
brain	way	creek	beet
chain		peek	feet
drain		seek	fleet
gain		week	greet
grain		eel	meet
main		feel	sheet
pain		heel	sleet
plain		peel	street
rain		steel	sweet
train		wheel	teeth
vain			
faint			
paint			
waist			
bait			
wait			

Vowel Digraphs
One-Syllable Words *cont.*

oa = ō	ea = ē		ea = ĕ
coach	flea	scream	bread
road	pea	steam	dead
load	sea	stream	head
toad	tea	team	lead
loaf	beach	bean	read
cloak	each	clean	spread
croak	peach	lean	thread
oak	preach	mean	tread
soak	reach	jeans	deaf
coal	teach	cheap	breast
foal	bead	heap	breath
goal	lead	leap	death
foam	read	clear	sweat
roam	leaf	dear	
groan	beak	ear	
loan	creak	hear	
moan	freak	near	
soap	peak	spear	
oar	sneak	year	
roar	speak	leash	
soar	weak	beast	
boat	deal	east	
coat	heal	feast	
float	meal	beat	
goat	real	cheat	
oat	seal	eat	
moat	steal	heat	
throat	beam	meat	
boast	cream	neat	
coast	dream	seat	
roast		treat	
toast		wheat	
coax			

Vowel Digraphs
Two-Syllable Words

ai = ā	ay = ā	ea = ē	ee = ē	oa = ō	ea = ĕ
afraid	away	appeal	agree	approach	ahead
await	betray	appear	asleep	charcoal	bedspread
complain	birthday	beacon	beehive	coaster	dreadful
contain	crayon	beaver	between	crossroad	feather
dainty	daydream	beneath	canteen	lifeboat	forehead
daily	delay	creature	cheerful	oatmeal	headline
daisy	display	defeat	coffee	overcoat	healthy
detail	driveway	eaten	degree	overload	heaven
exclaim	Friday	eager	fifteen	railroad	heavy
explain	haystack	leader	freedom	raincoat	instead
hailstone	highway	meanwhile	greedy	sailboat	leather
mailbox	layer	neatly	indeed	tugboat	peasant
mermaid	maybe	peacock	sixteen		pleasant
painful	mayor	peanut	succeed		ready
raindrop	pathway	reason	teepee		sweatband
remain	payment	repeat	weekday		weapon
tailor	playful	retreat	weeping		weather
traitor	raceway	seabird	Yankee		
	railway	season			
	relay	seaweed			
	Sunday	sneaker			
	subway	speaker			
		teacher			
		teaspoon			
		treaty			
		weaver			

Variant Vowel Digraphs and Diphthongs
One-Syllable Words

au (cause)	aw (law)	ew (new)	ie (die)	ie (brief)	oy (boy)	oi (boil)
cause	bawl	blew	die	brief	boy	boil
fault	claw	brew	lie	chief	joy	broil
fraud	crawl	chew	pie	field	Roy	choice
gauze	dawn	crew	tie	grief	soy	coil
haul	draw	dew		piece	toy	coin
launch	gnaw	drew		priest		foil
pause	hawk	few		shield		joint
sauce	jaw	flew		shriek		join
vault	law	grew		thief		noise
	lawn	knew		yield		oil
	paw	mew				point
	raw	new				soil
	saw	screw				spoil
	scrawl	stew				toil
	shawl	threw				voice
	straw					
	thaw					
	yawn					

Variant Vowel Digraphs and Diphthongs
One-Syllable Words, *cont.*

oo (boot)	oo (book)	ou (out)	ou (soup)	ow (cow)	ow (blow)
bloom	book	blouse	group	bow	blow
boom	brook	bounce	rouge	brow	blown
boost	cook	cloud	soup	brown	bow
boot	crook	couch	wound	clown	bowl
broom	foot	count	you	cow	crow
choose	good	crouch	youth	crowd	flow
cool	hood	doubt		crown	flown
droop	hook	flour		down	glow
food	look	found		drown	grow
fool	shook	ground		fowl	grown
goose	stood	house		frown	growth
groove	took	loud		gown	know
hoof	wood	mound		growl	low
hoop	wool	mount		how	mow
hoot		mouse		howl	owe
loop		mouth		now	own
loose		ouch		owl	row
moon		ounce		plow	show
noon		our		scowl	slow
pool		out		town	snow
proof		pouch		vow	throw
roof		pound			
room		pout			
root		proud			
school		round			
scoop		scout			
shoot		shout			
smooth		slouch			
soon		sound			
spool		sour			
spoon		south			
stool		spout			
stoop		sprout			
tool		trout			
tooth		wound			
troop					
zoo					

Variant Vowel Digraphs and Diphthongs
Two- Or More Syllable Words

au (cause)	aw (law)	ew (new)	ie (die)	ie (brief)
applause	awful	corkscrew	applied	babies
astronaut	awkward	curfew	dignified	belief
audio	awning	mildew	implied	believe
auditorium	crawfish	nephew	qualified	cashier
August	drawback	newspaper		grievance
author	drawbridge	screwdriver		handkerchief
authority	drawer	sewer		married
autograph	drawing			movies
automatic	lawful			rabies
because	lawyer			relief
cauliflower	lockjaw			varied
dinosaur	outlaw			
faucet	rawhide			
laundry	sawdust			
naughty	sawhorse			
nautical	scrawny			
overhaul	seesaw			
pauper	strawberry			
saucer	withdraw			
sausage				

Variant Vowel Digraphs and Diphthongs
Two- Or More Syllable Words, *cont.*

oy (boy)	oi (boil)	oo (boot)		oo (book)
annoy	avoid	afternoon	shampoo	barefoot
convoy	boiler	baboon	spoonful	childhood
decoy	disappoint	balloon	tattoo	falsehood
destroy	exploit	ballroom	toadstool	footprint
employ	moisture	bamboo	toothpaste	goodbye
enjoy	noisy	bassoon	trooper	handbook
loyal	ointment	bedroom	typhoon	motherhood
overjoy	poison	caboose	uproot	neighborhood
oyster	recoil	cartoon	whirlpool	outlook
royal	rejoice	cocoon		overlook
royalty	rejoin	gloomy		redwood
soybean	sirloin	harpoon		understood
tomboy	tinfoil	honeymoon		withstood
voyage	toilet	igloo		woodchuck
	turmoil	kangaroo		wooden
	typhoid	lagoon		woodland
		macaroon		woodpecker
		maroon		woolen
		monsoon		
		platoon		
		raccoon		
		rooftop		
		rooster		

Variant Vowel Digraphs and Diphthongs
Two- Or More Syllable Words, *cont.*

ou (out)

about	mouthful	
account	outlaw	
aground	outlet	
aloud	outline	
amount	outside	
announce	profound	
around	pronounce	
astound	rebound	
background	roundabout	
bloodhound	roundup	
boundary	southeast	
compound	surround	
devout	thousand	
discount	trousers	
doubt	underground	
fountain	without	
greyhound		
knockout		
loudspeaker		
mountain		

ou (soup)

acoustic
bouquet
caribou
cougar
coupon
routine
souvenir
youthful

ow (cow)

allow
breakdown
coward
cowboy
drowsy
flower
powder
power
powerful
shower
somehow
sundown
towel
tower
vowel
waterfowl

ow (blow)

arrow	shallow
bellows	snowball
below	sorrow
borrow	swallow
burrow	widow
disown	window
elbow	yellow
follow	
gallows	
hollow	
meadow	
mower	
narrow	
overblown	
overflow	
owner	
pillow	
rainbow	
scarecrow	
shadow	

ey (key)

abbey
alley
barley
chimney
donkey
galley
hockey
honey
jersey
jockey
kidney
money
monkey
parsley
trolley
turkey
valley

ey (they)

greyhound
heyday
obey
survey

Syllabication
Compound Words

airplane	fireworks
backache	flashlight
bedroom	football
barefoot	goldfish
footprint	homesick
checkup	lifeguard
downtown	lonesome
driveway	popcorn
earthquake	snowflake
eyelid	toothbrush
	weekend

Two-Syllable Words with Two Medial Consonants

cv̆c · cvc

absent	common	happen	pencil	success
attic	cotton	helmet	picnic	sudden
basket	custom	hidden	plastic	tablet
blanket	dentist	himself	possum	tennis
blossom	express	insect	problem	traffic
bottom	fallen	kidnap	public	triplet
button	funnel	kitten	puppet	trumpet
cactus	gallop	lesson	rabbit	tunnel
cannot	goblet	magnet	ribbon	upset
cobweb	gossip	mitten	signal	velvet
	gotten	napkin	splendid	

Two-Syllable Words with a Single Medial Consonant

C̄V · CVC

bacon	frozen	music	rival	Venus
began	gravy	nylon	robot	vital
clover	hotel	odor	ruler	vocal
cubic	item	omit	rumor	zebra
diner	July	paper	solar	
diver	label	pilot	spider	
driver	labor	protect	spoken	
favor	local	pupil	student	
fever	major	radar	tiger	
final	moment	recess	total	
flavor	motor	relax	tulip	

CV̆C · VC

cabin	legend	planet	talent
camel	lemon	polish	timid
city	level	project	visit
civil	limit	radish	wagon
clever	lizard	river	
closet	magic	robin	
comet	melon	salad	
comic	model	second	
credit	modern	seven	
digit	never	shiver	
dragon	panel	solid	
habit	pedal	spinach	
	petal	study	

Two-Syllable Words with Consonant Plus [le]

C̄V · C[le]

bible
bridle
bugle
cable
cradle
fable
ladle
maple
noble
rifle
stable
table
title

CV̆C · C[le]

battle	middle	sprinkle
bubble	muscle	struggle
bundle	paddle	stumble
candle	puddle	tickle
cattle	puzzle	tremble
dazzle	rattle	tumble
drizzle	riddle	uncle
fiddle	rumble	whistle
gentle	saddle	wiggle
giggle	settle	
handle	simple	
jingle	single	
jungle	smuggle	

Words with Prefixes

dis	im	in	mis	pre
disagree	impatient	inactive	misbehave	prearrange
disappear	imperfect	incomplete	mislay	precook
disarm	impolite	incorrect	mislead	prepaid
disconnect	impossible	indefinite	misplace	preschool
dishonest	impure		mispronounce	pretest
dislike			misread	preview
disloyal			misspell	
dismount			mistreat	
disobey			misuse	
disorder				
disown				
distrust				

re

reappear	remove
rearm	rename
rearrange	renumber
recount	repack
redo	repaint
reenter	repay
refill	replace
refresh	replay
refried	reread
regrew	rerun
regroup	resale
reheat	reshape
rehire	retell
reload	rethink
remade	retrace
remake	reword
remarry	rewrite

un

unable	unheated
unafraid	unkind
unbroken	unknown
uncertain	unlike
uncommon	unlock
uncooked	unlucky
uncover	unpainted
undecided	unreal
undress	unselfish
unequal	untangle
uneven	untied
unexpected	unusual
unfair	unwrapped
unfamiliar	
unfasten	
unhappy	
unhealthy	

Words with Suffixes

ful

careful
cheerful
colorful
delightful
disgraceful
fearful
forgetful
armful
helpful
hopeful
joyful
painful
peaceful
playful
respectful
restful
successful
thankful
useful
wasteful
wonderful
youthful

less

ageless
beardless
blameless
breathless
careless
childless
cloudless
fearless
harmless
helpless
homeless
hopeless
jobless
painless
restless
sleepless
useless
worthless

ly

badly
bravely
brightly
cleverly
fairly
foolishly
freely
gladly
greatly
happily
honestly
kindly
lonely
loudly
nearly
neatly
nervously
politely
proudly
quietly
rudely
safely
sickly
smoothly
softly
sweetly
swiftly
wisely

ness

cleverness
darkness
fairness
foolishness
goodness
greatness
kindness
likeness
loudness
meanness
nervousness
politeness
sadness
sickness
smoothness
softness
sweetness
swiftness
thickness

er

bomber
catcher
commander
dancer
defender
designer
dodger
driver
dryer
explorer
follower
gambler
golfer
invader
juggler
leader
manager
painter
performer
pitcher
pointer
rancher
robber
ruler
scraper
settler
sharpener
shopper
speaker
stinger
teacher
trapper
washer

or

actor
calculator
collector
conductor
decorator
dictator
governor
inspector
inventor
operator
protector
survivor
visitor

Words with Suffixes, *cont.*

ment

agreement
amazement
announcement
arrangement
development
employment
entertainment
excitement
payment
punishment
shipment
treatment

en

blacken
brighten
cheapen
dampen
darken
fatten
flatten
freshen
gladden
golden
harden
lengthen
lighten
loosen
moisten
quicken
ripen
sadden
sharpen
shorten
strengthen
sweeten
thicken

tighten
toughen
whiten
widen
wooden

ion

action
attraction
celebration
collection
communication
construction
correction
decoration
demonstration
destruction
digestion
direction
election
graduation
hibernation
infection
injection
inspection
invention
location
migration
objection
operation
pollution
protection
rotation
selection
suggestion
vacation
collision
confusion
decision

discussion
division
erosion
explosion

ible

collapsible
collectible
convertible
defensible
digestible
expressible
forcible
reversible

able

admirable
agreeable
approachable
avoidable
believable
breakable
comfortable
curable
desirable
enjoyable
excitable
excusable
exchangable
imaginable
laughable
likeable
manageable
moveable
noticeable
observable
pleasurable
readable

replaceable
respectable
salable
teachable
trainable
understandable
usable
washable
wearable
workable

Words with Multiple Affixes

breathlessness	immovable	removable	unselfishness
carelessly	impatiently	repayable	unsinkable
carelessness	imperfectly	repayment	unsuccessful
cheerfulness	incompletely	replacement	unthinkable
disagreement	incorrectly	restlessness	usefulness
disgraceful	indecision	reusable	
dishonorable	inexcusable	unbelievable	
disorderly	miscommunication	uncomfortable	
disrespectful	mistreatment	unfairly	
fearlessly	prepayment	unforgettable	
forgetfulness	reaction	unfriendly	
hopefully	rearrangement	ungrateful	
hopelessness	reelection	unnoticeable	

Words Containing Vowel Patterns

all	alt	igh and ight		ild	ind
ball	asphalt	bright	moonlight	child	behind
baseball	cobalt	candlelight	night	mild	bind
call	halt	daylight	right	wild	find
downfall	halter	delight	sigh		grind
fall	malt	fight	sight		hind
football	salt	flight	slight		kind
hall	waltz	fright	starlight		mankind
install		frighten	sunlight		mind
mall		high	thigh		wind
nightfall		highway	tight		
rainfall		knight	tighten		
recall		lamplight	twilight		
small		light			
snowball		lightning			
squall		midnight			
stall		might			
tall					
wall					
waterfall					

Words Containing Vowel Patterns, *cont.*

old		olt	ost
blindfold	mold	bolt	almost
bold	old	colt	compost
cold	scold	jolt	ghost
fold	sold	revolt	host
foothold	told	volt	most
gold	unfold		post
hold	untold		
household	withhold		

Words with Vowel Letter [a] Preceded by [w]

wa (warm)	wa (wasp)
walk	swallow
wall	swamp
walnut	swan
walrus	swap
waltz	swat
war	wad
warble	waffle
ward	wallet
warden	wallop
warm	wampum
warmth	wander
warn	wasp
warning	watch
warp	watchdog
warship	watt
water	
watermelon	
waterproof	

Glossary

abstract words   words describing a quality (e.g., *dependable*), feeling (*sadness*), or idea (*democracy*).

affix   a general term used to refer to both prefixes and suffixes. See also **prefix** and **suffix.**

alliteration   the repetition, usually, of initial consonant sounds in a series of words. Tongue twisters are popular examples of alliteration: Peter Piper picked a peck of pickled peppers.

alphabetic language   a language in which significant speech sounds are assigned printed equivalents which form the written record of the language.

alphabetic principle   the basic understanding in an alphabetic writing system that each significant speech sound has its own graphic counterpart. See also **alphabetic language.**

analogy   the correspondence or similarity between pairs or sets of words. In reading, the process of analogous reasoning involves discovering the similarity and using that to decode similar new words. For example, discovering the similarity in *make* and *cake* and using knowledge of initial consonants, the reader can decode words such as *bake, fake, Jake, lake, rake, sake, take,* and *wake*.

analytic approach   a method for teaching letter-sound correspondences that begins by separating the sounds and letters of known words: *met = m-e-t.*

at risk   a term used to describe children who have unusual difficulties in learning because of one or more factors, including language deficits, learning disabilities, or below-average intelligences.

auditory blending   combining separate phonemes or speech sounds after they are heard and pronouncing them as whole words: /t/ /o/ /p/ = *top.* Research studies have found that auditory blending ability in kindergarten and grade 1 is a significant predictor of future reading achievement.

auditory discrimination   recognizing likenesses and differences in speech sounds: *dig–down* (likeness); *dig–pig* (difference).

automatic identification   the quick, sure recognition of words without the need for detailed analysis. See also **sight words.**

base word   often used interchangeably with **root word**. Base words may be free or bound morphemes to which affixes or inflectional endings may be added. For example, *cat* (a free morpheme—can stand alone) is the base word in *cats,* and *trieve* (a bound morpheme—cannot stand alone) is the base word in *retrieve.* See also **root word.**

beginning letter substitution strategy   an early teaching activity that focuses on changing the initial consonants of words to help the reader decode them.

blending   see **auditory blending** and **phonic blending.**

code-breaking   see **decoding.**

code emphasis approach   a beginning reading method that emphasizes mastery of the alphabetic code; that is, learning and using letter-sound correspondences to identify words, rather than the meaning of the text. See **meaning emphasis approach.**

cognition   the act or process by which a person comes to know something.

compound words   words made up of two or more words that can occur alone, for example: *football, lighthouse.*

consonant blend   a sequence of two or more consonants in a word, each of which retains and preserves its distinct sound when the word is pronounced. The group of letters is often referred to as a **consonant combination** or consonant cluster and the resulting sound as a blend. Consonant blends can occur in an initial or final position:

tr	str	st	sk	nd	nt
train	*strike*	*stop*	*skate*	*band*	*bent*
		best	*ask*		

consonant combination   see **consonant blend** and **consonant digraph.**

consonant digraph   a sequence of two consonant letters that represents a single speech sound different from either consonant sound alone. Consonant digraphs can occur in an initial or final position:

ch	sh	th (voiceless)	th (voiced)	wh
check	*ship*	*thing*	*this*	*whale*
pinch	*fish*	*both*	*bathe*	

consonant letters   letters that represent the consonant sounds; all letters that are not vowels: [b], [c], [d], [f], [g], [h], [j], [k], [l], [m], [n], [p], [q], [r], [s], [t], [v], [w], [x], [y], and [z]. See also **consonant sounds.**

consonants or consonant sounds   the speech sounds that are the result of partial or near complete blockage of the flow of air as it passes through the speaker's breath channel. They are represented by the consonant letters, singly or in combination; e.g., /s/ and /t/ represented by the single letters [s] and [t], and /sh/ and /ch/ represented by the letter combinations [sh] and [ch].

context   the words and sentences surrounding an unfamiliar word that offer clues to its pronunciation and/or meaning. See **semantic clues** and **syntax.**

continuants   vowels and certain consonant sounds that can be continued or prolonged without being altered: /f/, /v/, /h/, /s/, /z/, /sh/, /r/, /m/, /n/, /l/, /w/, voiced and voiceless /th/, and the vowels are commonly thought of as continuants but /r/ and /w/ may be challenged by some linguists.

conventional spelling   the accepted spelling of a word according to a dictionary. See also **invented spelling.**

cryptologists or **cryptographers**   people who study, write, or decipher codes or ciphers.

curriculum   a carefully constructed course of study.

CVC   a symbol used to indicate a word or syllable that follows the consonant-vowel-consonant pattern.

CVC   CVC CVC

bat   *bit/ten*

CVC[e]   a symbol used to indicate a word or syllable that follows the consonant-vowel-consonant-final [e] pattern.

CVC[e]   CV/CVC[e]

gate   *fi/nite*

decoding   a term frequently used to describe the process of converting the printed word into its spoken form. When students **decode** a written word, they may use their knowledge of letter-sound relationships and/or word parts (e.g., affixes and inflectional endings). This activity is also referred to as **code-breaking, ciphering,** or **sounding out.**

dialects   regional variations of a language. They may include differences in vocabulary, grammar, and/or pronunciation.

diphthong   a vowel sound made up of two adjoining and identifiable vowel sounds in the same syllable; for example: the vowel sounds in *cloud, oil, how, oyster*. Each of the vowels contributes to the final sound produced. Sometimes it is referred to as a vowel blend.

dysfluent reading   reading characterized by hesitation, the opposite of fluency. See **fluency.**

dyslexia   according to the Orton Dyslexia Society, this word is defined as a neurologically-based, often familial, disorder which interferes with the acquisition and processing of language. Varying in degrees of severity, it is manifested by difficulties in receptive and expressive language, including phonological processing, reading, writing, spelling, hand-writing, and sometimes arithmetic.

emergent literacy   an early stage in the development of "conventional" literacy in which children explore and develop the various skills involved in reading and writing.

encoding   a term that describes the process of converting spoken words into their written forms. See **decoding.**

English phonology and orthography   according to most authorities, English phonology (system of sounds) consists of approximately forty-four different sounds or phonemes. Using an alphabet of twenty-six let-ters, English orthography (writing) represents these forty-four sounds with either single letters or combinations of letters. For this reason the letter-sound correspondences in English are more complicated than in some other languages.

fluency   the flow while reading smoothly and at a normal rate without word recognition difficulties. See **dysfluent reading.**

geminate consonants   a pair of identical consonants that represents the same sound as the single consonant letter. In some instances (e.g., *funny*) the presence of these doubled letter may result in the sound being prolonged. In others it may have no consequence (e.g., *dull*).

indirect, incidental, informal phonics   an approach to teaching phonics that uses "the appropriate moment" during reading and writing activities to convey relationships between letters and sounds. The terms **indi-rect, incidental,** and **informal** are often used interchangeably and contrasted with **systematic, explicit,** and **direct.** See **systematic, explicit, direct phonic instruction.**

individualized reading program   an approach to reading in which the students select their own material (usually trade books) and read them at their own pace. The teacher may assign skill instruction on the basis of classroom observations and student conferences.

inflectional endings   affixes added to the end of words to indicate number (noun affixes—*ox/oxen, snake/snakes, bush/bushes*) or tense (verb affixes—*playing, plays, played*). These endings are added to base words. The word inflectional is sometimes spelled inflexional.

integrated language arts curriculum   a program of instruction and learning that com-bines activities in reading, writing, spelling, speaking, and listening.

invented spelling   the spelling of words according to the sounds heard in the words—most often used by young children with a limited knowledge of sound-symbol relationships. Any given sound is often represented by a letter whose name contains a similar sound. Thus *water* may be spelled with a [y] representing the /w/ sound, an [o] for the vowel sound and [tr] for the remainder of the word: yotr. Invented spelling has been incorporated in instructional techniques for beginning reading and according to proponents of the technique, young writers will eventually make a transition from these initial approximations to conventional spelling. This practice is sometimes referred to as personal or temporary spelling.

kinesthetic method   an approach to letter-word recognition that advocates the physical tracing of large letters and words simultaneously pronouncing the sounds in the words. The kinesthetic or VAKT method integrates visual (seeing the word), auditory (hearing the word), and kinesthetic-tactile (tracing the word) modes of learning. It was developed by Grace Fernald and others in the early 1940s.

language experience reading program   a reading approach for beginners in which the students' own experiences as well as classroom discussions are transcribed by the teacher, displayed, and used as the reading text.

learning disabilities   See **dyslexia.**

letter-sound   correspondence   the connection between a specific letter (grapheme) and a specific sound (phoneme); for example, the letter [s] and the sound /s/ as heard at the beginning of the word seal. This connection is also referred to as a symbol-sound or grapheme-phoneme correspondence, association, or relationship.

linguistic patterns   spelling patterns that relate to pronunciation and are included in a single syllable. For example, [an] as in pan, [ame] as in tame, [aim] as in claim, etc. See also **phonograms.**

listening vocabulary   the words a person understands or knows when they are heard.

literacy   the ability to read and write.

literature-based reading program   an approach to reading in which trade or library books representing the broad spectrum of literature serve as the core texts.

long vowels   a term used to describe the vowel sounds that are the same as the names of the alphabet letters [a], [e], [i], [o], and [u]. Long vowels occur in words and stressed syllables ending in a final silent [e]: save, de/cide. They also occur in words or stressed syllables ending in a single vowel: she, mu/sic. Long vowel sounds may also be represented by more than one letter, as in aim, peach, or boat. See **vowel digraphs, magic [e] rule.**

magic [e] rule   a phonic generalization based on the CVC[e] spelling pattern. According to this rule, when a short word ends with an [e], the preceding vowel represents these long vowel sounds and the final [e] is silent. For example: /ā/ as in *late*, /ī/ in *five*, and /ō/ in *stone*. See **CVC[e].**

meaning emphasis approach   a beginning reading method that places the primary focus of instruction on the meaning of the text, that is, on reading and reacting to what is read, rather than on learning to decode. See **code emphasis approach.**

meaning vocabulary   a term used to describe the number of words that a student controls or knows. In general, the more extensively a person reads, the greater his or her meaning vocabulary will be.

medial vowels   vowel letters and sounds which appear between two (or more) consonants, for example: *ten, string, brush*.

miscues   misreadings in oral reading.

morpheme   the smallest meaningful unit in a language. It cannot be subdivided without the loss of its original meaning. Morphemes can be free or bound. The word *dog* is a free morpheme because it can stand alone. On the other hand the word *dogs* contains two morphemes—*dog* and the inflectional ending [s]. The [s] is a bound morpheme, and indicates plurality, but cannot occur alone.

murmur vowel   see **schwa.**

neurologically-based reading difficulties   reading disabilities that, in the opinion of some authorities, may be caused by differences in the brain.

noun inflections   see **inflectional endings.**

orthography   the system of written language that represents human speech; spelling. It includes the correct formation of letters used to represent sounds as well as the correct spellings of words.

picture clues   see **visual clues.**

philologists   people who study language in a historical and comparative context with a particular emphasis on uncovering word origins and the true meaning of written records.

phonemes   the minimal speech sounds in a language that differentiate one word from another (/r/ /e/ /d/ in *red*, /b/ /ī/ /k/ in *bike*). The exact number of phonemes in English is debatable. Some authorities claim there are about 32 standard English phonemes while others have identified as many as 44.

phonemic awareness   an early interest in and growing facility with the sounds of a language. This facility includes the ability to detect rhymes, segment and blend sounds in spoken words, and to manipulate sounds in words through phoneme addition and/or deletion.

phonic blending   the ability to act on a printed word, breaking it into parts, giving each letter or letter combination its corresponding sound, and pronouncing the word.

phonic elements   a comprehensive term that includes various categories of speech sounds such as vowels, consonants, consonant blends, and diphthongs.

phonic generalizations   rules about common spelling-pronunciation patterns.

phonics   the study and use of symbol-sound (grapheme-phoneme) relationships to help students identify written words.

phonograms   groupings of letters, usually consisting of a vowel and a final consonant, that can be used by students to write and read new words. These new words are created through the substitution of initial consonants, consonant clusters, and digraphs: e.g., using the phonogram [ip], from *tip* to *rip* (initial consonant), *slip* (consonant cluster), *chip* (digraph). Phonograms have also been referred to as **linguistic patterns**, spelling patterns, word families, or graphemic bases.

phonology   the sound system of a language. See **English phonology and orthography.**

picture clues   see **visual clues.**

polysyllabic word   a word containing more than one syllable. It is also referred to as a multisyllabic word.

prefix   a word element (a bound morpheme), that can be added to the beginning of a word forming a new word with a different meaning; for example: *mislead, reprint, untie.* The general term **affix** is used for both prefixes and suffixes.

print concepts   basic ideas related to written language such as letter, word, sentence, and story that young readers need to understand as part of the beginning reading process.

rate of reading   the speed at which a person reads. The term usually applies to silent reading. Among the factors affecting the rate of reading are the reader's ability, complexity of the material, familiarity with the subject matter, the style of the writing, and the purpose for reading the text.

reading comprehension   an understanding of the text that is read. The skill ranges from a literal understanding of a text to a more critical-creative appreciation of it.

reading disability   a term used to describe difficulty in learning to read, i.e., reading below potential.

reading readiness   a term describing both the skills and knowledge necessary to undertake learning to read and the assessment of a pupil's preparedness for reading. See **emergent literacy,** a term also used to describe the development of these skills and knowledge.

Reading Recovery   an early intervention program designed to help young readers through intensive tutorial sessions.

rhyme   the correspondence in the terminal sound units of words. For example, *cap/map/tap* rhyme because they share the same final sound unit. Rhyming words consist of an initial consonant or consonant cluster called the <u>onset</u> and a terminal sound unit called the <u>rhyme</u> (also <u>rime</u>).

root word   the simplest form of a word when all prefixes, suffixes, and inflectional endings have been stripped away. It carries the main meaning of the word and can be used to create related words, for example: *re<u>move</u>, <u>move</u>able, <u>move</u>s*. A root word is also referred to as a <u>stem</u> or **base word.**

rote learning learning that has been viewed as relying mainly on memory as compared with problem solving.

schwa   the vowel sound heard in an unstressed syllable. It is represented by various graphic symbols: [a] in *away*, [o] in *gallop*, [u] in *circus*. The schwa is also referred to as a **murmur vowel** or <u>neutral vowel</u> and *∂* is its pronunciation symbol.

segmenting   the division of a word into its component phonemes or speech sounds.

semantic clues information contained in the meaning of words, phrases, and sentences that helps the reader to identify unfamiliar words. See **syntactic clues.**

short vowels   a term used to describe the vowel sounds represented by the /a/ in *crab*, /e/ in *bed*, /i/ in *ship*, /o/ in *top*, and /u/ in *plug*.

sight words   those words recognized immediately or automatically on sight without the need for word analysis. Many words previously learned through decoding become sight words as the result of repeated exposure. Other words such as *the, of,* and *said* are generally taught as sight words because of their frequency and phonic irregularity.

silent letter the letter or letters in a word that are not pronounced, for example: *com<u>b</u>, <u>k</u>nife, ni<u>ght</u>*.

sounding out see **phonic blending.**

speaking vocabulary the words that individuals use to express themselves orally. The speaking vocabulary of a primary school child is likely to be ten times greater than the reading vocabulary.

spelling pattern approach   see **phonograms.**

structural analysis a term used to describe various aspects of the written language with which a reader interacts as part of an overall word identification strategy. These structural features include compound words, plural forms, inflectional endings, affixes, syllabication, and contractions.

suffix   a word element (letter or syllable) added to the end of a word. Derivational suffixes form new words with different meanings: *use* + less = *useless*; *short* + age = *shortage*. Inflectional suffixes modify the grammatical function of the word: *ox* + en = *oxen* (plural); *write* + s = *writes* (present tense). The general term **affix** is used for both prefixes and suffixes.

syllable   a word or part of a word pronounced as a unit. A syllable usually contains a vowel.

syllabication   the division of a word into syllables. It provides the reader with information on how to pronounce the word. The word syllabification is often used with the same meaning.

syllabic generalizations   rules that help a reader divide an unknown word into syllables in order to identify it. These guidelines allow the student to approach a new word with a flexible problem-solving strategy.

syntax   the arrangement of words and inflectional endings that signal word relationships within a sentence. Skillful readers use syntactic features along with other clues to help them identify unfamiliar words and understand the text.

synthetic approach   a method in which the individual letter-sound correspondences are taught and then blended to form words: /b/ /at/ /th/ = *bath*. See also **phonic blending.**

systematic, explicit, direct phonic instruction   a method in which the teacher directly presents the letter-sound correspondences according to a carefully structured curriculum. In this approach to teaching phonics the terms systematic, explicit, and direct are often interchangeable.

technical words   words that are part of the specialized vocabulary of a curriculum area, discipline, or profession; for example, *denominator* in mathematics, *byte* in computer studies, *habeas corpus* in law.

verb inflection   see **inflectional endings.**

visual clues   distinctive letter forms, word configurations, or illustrations (pictures) which readers can use to help them identify an unknown word.

vocabulary   see **listening vocabulary, meaning vocabulary,** and **speaking vocabulary.**

voiced and voiceless /th/   two different sounds represented by the consonant digraph [th]. The voiced /th/ corresponds to the sound heard in *this, that,* and *the.* The voiceless /th/ corresponds to the sound heard in such words as *thing, think,* and *thin.*

vowel combinations   see **diphthongs** and **vowel digraphs.**

vowel digraph   a sequence of two vowels that represent long vowel sounds or diphthongs, for example: *meal, goat, snail, snow, cloud.*

vowels   speech sounds produced by the unobstructed flow of air through the speaker's breath channel. Every syllable contains a vowel.

vowel letters   the letters used singly or in combination to represent the vowel sounds: [a], [e], [i], [o], [u], and [y].

vowels with [r]   a vowel sound followed by an /r/ that is different from either a long or a short vowel sound. The letters [er] in *germ*, [ir] in *bird,* and [ur] in *hurt* all stand for the same /ər/ sound. The letters [ar] represent the sound /är/ heard in *car*, or the sound /ôr/ heard in *fort*.

whole language   an educational movement founded in the 1970s but with historical antecedents. It advocates integrated language arts instruction, adopts an incidental approach to phonics instruction, and encourages the use of writing using invented spelling as a way to reinforce letter-sound relationships. The philosophy and practices of whole language are also referred to by the terms **literature-based reading program** or **integrated language arts curriculum.**

word analysis   a comprehensive term used to describe the various strategies employed by readers to identify words. Chief among the strategies are phonic analysis, structural analysis, and, to a lesser degree, word shape clues. It is also referred to as word attack.

word families   see **phonograms.**

word identification   see **word recognition.**

word recognition   the strategies employed to identify words. Some reading authorities use word identification and word recognition interchangeably.

Index

Almy, Millie, 37
Alphabet, 4, 9
   teaching strategy for recognizing,
      naming, and writing, 67–68
Alphabetic writing, 4–5
   assessing, 90–92
Alternate consonant sounds: soft [c]
      and [g] words, list of, 122
Applying phonic skills and knowledge,
      21–22
Assessing student progress, 89–103
   alphabetic writing, 90–92
   general guidelines, 89–90
   letter-to-sound associations, 93–103
   phonemic awareness, 92–93
   print concepts, 90
Associating consonant letters with
      sounds at beginning of words,
      assessment of, 93
Auditory blending, 69–70

Beginning consonant blends,
      assessment of, 95–96
Beginning letters of words, teaching
      strategy for, 71
Beginning sounds in words, teaching
      strategy for, 70–71

Bissex, Glenda, 37
Blending sounds, 6

Chomsky, Carol, 37
Classroom atmosphere, 21, 22
Comparatives, 62
Consonant blends, 44–45
   teaching strategy, 76
Consonant combinations, 13
Consonant digraphs, 47–48, 96–97
   blends, 49
   teaching strategy, 76–77
Consonant letter-to-sound
      correspondences, 16
Consonants, 41–42
   teaching strategy
      consonant substitution to read
        and write new words,
        73–74
      letter-sound associations at
        beginnings of words, 71–72
      soft [c] and [g] generalization,
        72–73
Consonant substitution
   assessing, 93–94
   teaching strategy, 73–74
Contractions, 61

CVC (consonant-vowel-consonant)
   words, 43
   assessment of, 94–95

Decoding, 2, 3
Durkin, Dolores, 37

English as a second language, 12
Errors in oral reading, 16, 25, 26

Final geminate (double) consonants
   and [ck], 46
First grade phonics program, 18

Generalizations (rules), 12–13

Indirect phonics, 7
   effectiveness of, 7, 8, 9
Inflected endings, list of words with,
   130–131
Invented spelling, 37

Kindergarten phonics program, 18
Kinesthetic approach, 107–108

Letter-sound correspondences, 6–10
Linguistic patterns, 108–110
Long vowels, 17
   at end of words or syllables, 51
   list of words with, 125
Long vowels with final [e], 50–51
   words ending in [ve], 51
Long vowel words with final [e]
   assessing, 97–98
   list of words, 123–125
   teaching strategy, 77–78

Magic [e] rule, 50, 78
Manipulating sounds in words, 70
Meaning, and phonics, 2–3
Medial vowels, hearing
   letter-sound associations, 75
   teaching strategy, 74–75

Miscues, 7, 22
Modified phonic blending approach,
   109–111
Morphemes, 10
Multiple affixes, list of words with,
   146

Noun inflections—plurals, 56
   teaching strategy, 81

Oral phonics work, 21
Order of teaching and learning phonic
   elements, 40
Overuse of phonics by students, 32

Phonemes, 9
Phonemic awareness, 4, 31
   assessing, 92–93
   teaching strategy
      auditory blending, 69–70
      manipulating sounds in words,
         70
      rhyming, 68–69
Phonic blending approach, 31
Phonic instruction, 6–9, 21–27
   effective program, 21–22, 28
   indirect, incidental, informal
      method, 7
   objectives and teaching strategies,
      24
   phonics and other word
      identification skills, 25–27
   prereading and early reading
      strategies, 25–26
   syllabication, 26–27
   place of sight words, 24–25
   systematic, explicit, direct method,
      6–7
   textbooks, workbooks, and teacher-
      made material, 23
   time given to, 22–23
   whole-class, group, and individual
      instruction, 23

Phonic knowledge, and reading
      comprehension, 1–2
Phonics checklist, 103, 104
Phonics in total reading program,
      34–39
   language, cognition, and word
      identification, 34–35
   phonics and whole language
      programs, 35–36
   relationship between
      writing/spelling and phonics,
      37–38
   why some phonics programs fail, 38
Phonics programs
   kindergarten, 18
   first grade, 18
   second grade, 19
   third (and fourth) grades, 19
Phonograms, teaching strategy for, 73
Polysyllabic words, 2
Possessives, 61
Predictable stories, 107
Prefixes, 64
   list of words with, 143
   teaching strategy, 86–88
Prereading and early reading
      strategies, 25–26
Print concepts
   assessing, 90
   teaching strategies
      the alphabet, capital letters, and
         lowercase letters, 67
      stories, sentences, words, letters,
         66–67

Read, Charles, 37
Reading, meaningful, 3
Reading comprehension, 1–2
Reading programs, place of phonics in,
      34–39
Reading Recovery program, 9
Reading strategies, prereading and
      early reading, 25–26

Remedial instruction, 103, 105–106,
      112
Remedial reading programs, and
      phonics, 9
Research on phonics, 1–2, 7–8, 16, 23
Rhyming, 68–69

Schwa, 64
   vowel letters [a] and [o] preceded by
      [w], 54
   vowel letters [a] and [u] followed by
      [l], 54
Second grade phonics program, 19
Sequence for teaching phonic
      elements, 16–17
Short vowels, 17, 43
   list of words with, 113–121
Sight words, 24–25, 106–107
Silent consonants, 55–56
   list of words with, 129
   teaching strategy, 80–81
Single consonants, 13
Single vowels, 13
"Sounding out" words, 3, 13, 18, 21
Sounds of language, 4
Spelling, relationship to phonics,
      37–38
Spelling pattern approach, 31
Spelling-to-sound correspondences, 9,
      10, 12
Students
   and interest in learning phonics,
      4–5
   and knowledge of phonics, 11–15
      concepts to be understood, 12
      knowledge and use of letter-sound
         correspondences and
         generalizations, 12–13
      letter substitution strategies, 14
      positive attitude toward, 14–15
      practice in using, 14
      prerequisite skills and abilities,
         11–12

Students having difficulties with
phonics/reading
alternative approaches for,
105–112
kinesthetic approach, 108
linguistic patterns, 108–110
modified phonic blending
approach, 109–112
visual approach, 106
visual-motor approach, 107
identifying, 29–30
students who overuse phonics, 32
teaching phonics to children with
difficulty reading, 30–31
assessing underlying skills, 31
phonic blending approach, 31
spelling pattern approach, 31
teaching prerequisite phonic skills,
31
Suffixes
list of words with, 144–145
teaching strategy, 86–88
Syllabication, 26–27, 59–61
assessing, 102–103
teaching strategy
CV/CVC and CVC/VC words,
84–85
CVC/CVC words, 78–79
words ending in c[le], 85
word lists, 140–142
Syllabic generalizations, 10
Syllables in words, hearing, teaching
strategy for, 78
Systematic phonics, 6–7
effectiveness of, 7–9

Teacher-made material, 23
Teachers, and phonics fundamentals,
9–11
Teaching phonics, 6–9
Teaching strategies, 66–88
Textbooks, 23

Third (and fourth) grade phonics
program, 19
Trachtenburg, Phyllis, 36
Two-syllable words with digraphs,
teaching, 85–86

Variant vowel digraphs and
diphthongs, 62–63
lists of words with, 135–139
teaching strategy, 83–84
Verb inflections—[ed], [ing], [s], 57
teaching strategy, 82
Visual approach, 106–107
predictable stories, 107
sight words, 106–107
Visual-motor approach, 108
Vowel digraphs, 10, 13, 58
assessing, 99–102
list of words with, 132–134
teaching strategy, 82–83
Vowel letter-to-sound correspondences,
17
Vowel patterns, list of words
containing, 147–148
Vowels followed by [r], 13, 53
assessing, 98–99
list of words with, 127–128
teaching strategy, 80

Whole language programs, and
phonics, 35–36
Word analysis
comparatives, 62
contractions, 61
noun inflections—plurals, 56
possessives, 61
verb inflections—[ed], [ing], [s], 57
Word identification, 1, 2
related to reading comprehension, 1
Word lists, 113–148
Word patterns, 65, 88
assessing, 103

Word recognition, 2
Workbooks, 23
Writing, and relationship to phonics,
    37–38

[y] as a vowel, 52
    list of words with, 126
    teaching strategy, 79–80